THE DUCHESS OF KENT

Helen Cathcart

THE DUCHESS OF KENT

W. H. ALLEN . LONDON . 1971

Printed and bound in Great Britain
by The Garden City Press Limited,
Letchworth, Hertfordshire SG6 IJS
for the publishers
W. H. Allen and Co. Ltd
A Division of Howard & Wyndham Ltd.

ISBN 0 491 00438 9

Contents

The chapter sub-headings are from the original lyrics to the tunes played by the chimes of the grandfather clock on the staircase at Hovingham Hall.

Illustrations

Author's Note

Today's Duchess of Kent—the former Miss Katharine Worsley—is a comparative newcomer to the royal scene, and this first biographical study could not have been completed without the courtesy and help of various members of the Worsley family and other close relatives and friends. They gave material assistance in furnishing specific information, discerning comment and invaluable correction, and the author offers most grateful acknowledgement and thanks.

I am similarly indebted to Mr George Howard, Miss Christian Howard and Miss Barbara E. Baker, Comptroller of Castle Howard; to Miss B. D. Snape, headmistress of Queen Margaret's School, and her colleague, Miss Brenda Bridges, with other members of the staff, and to Miss M. L. Kilvert, headmistress of Runton Hill.

Mr Justin Wintle of Magdalen College made many enquiries on my behalf in Oxford, and I am particularly appreciative of the further assistance there of Miss A. E. Hubler, Mrs W. R. Schiele and Mr A. T. Brown. At a later stage, Patricia, Lady Eden, kindly accorded me fuller information on the days when the Duchess of Kent was a helper at her Kensington school. Mr W. G. Matters of the *Toronto Star* and Miss C. M. Lapointe of Montreal greatly assisted me with research in Canada, and I am again indebted to Mr Harold A. Albert for his tireless persistence in enabling me to draw so many factual threads together.

Mr G. P. Knowles, legal secretary to the Archbishop of York, contributed the benefit of his great legal knowledge, and Miss Dorothy Hudson of the North Riding County Library went to endless trouble to provide material on the Hovingham Festivals, while I am also under an obligation to Miss K. H. Wint, senior assistant archivist of the North Riding of Yorkshire County Record Office, who first drew my attention to the Worsley family records.

It would be difficult to thank all the executive officials of the charities and other organizations with which Her Royal Highness is connected who have kindly given information. Assistance has come from sources as varied as the Hong Kong Government Office in London and the Ministry of Defence. Not least, however, I must not omit my thanks to the ever-helpful staff of the B.B.C. Music Library for their skill in enabling me to trace the eighteenth century lyrics of the tunes chimed through the year by the grandfather clock at Hovingham Hall.

HELEN CATHCART

1 The Birthday Baby

This great World is a Trouble,
Where all must their fortunes bear;
Make the most of the Bubble,
You'll have but a Neighbour's fare ...

Sung by Mr D'Legard in *Jupiter and Europa*
(The February chimes of the Hovingham clock)

I

Today's Duchess of Kent, the former Katharine Worsley, was born during a snowstorm. She was born into a muted, white-cloaked world early on the morning of February 22nd, 1933, at Hovingham Hall, in the North Riding of Yorkshire, and, within minutes, the echo of her first cry in that solid mansion met the responsive chimes of the grandfather clock on the staircase, sweetly moving through a popular eighteenth century air. The baby Katharine was moreover born on her brother Oliver's birthday, the first girl in a family of boys, a charming blue-eyed keepsake for her parents in their ninth year of marriage.

"This great World is a Trouble", claimed the clock, playing its second tune of the year. Not an auspicious thought, if anyone knew the lyric, but the old clock had reiterated the theme ever since the Hall had been built, every hour every February for nearly two hundred years. The movement was made by John Ellicott, a London clockmaker of the reign of George II, and, so far as any member of the Worsley family remembered to regulate the semicircular dial, the chimes played a different tune for every month of the year, tinkling in early spring through Mr Handel's marches and minuets and sustaining the hours of summer and autumn with the refrains of forgotten old-time ballads and the choicest of Mr Gay's songs from *The Beggar's Opera*.

The early arrival of the baby aroused the household, but the news presumably travelled last of all to her three brothers, Marcus, Oliver and John, asleep in their nursery wing at the far southern end of the house. Aged seven, six and four, they awoke to the tidings of a baby sister and the excitement of discovering that the snowstorm had covered the lawns and yews with sugar-icing. Oliver opened the greeting-cards and gifts of his sixth birthday, and the three were taken to see the new baby with many a "Shush!" from Nanny Mist and many an agitated rustle of her white starched apron and, accustomed only to brothers, they tiptoed to the cot with infinite caution and "a kind of wonderment". When hinting to one or two friends the previous autumn that his wife anticipated another child, Captain "Willy" Worsley had made no secret of his hopes for a daughter. With his eldest boy, indeed, seven-year-old Marcus, shortly leaving the nest for prep school, the wish for a little girl about the house appeared an appropriate boon to seek of a benevolent providence.

At about breakfast time, the local Dr Kininmoth came down the staircase to tell the proud father—and the baby's grandfather, Sir William Henry Worsley—that everything was reassuringly satisfactory with mother and child. It seemed too early for champagne but, as head of the house, old Sir William soon insisted on broaching a symbolic bottle, "To my grand-daughter—to the baby, to her long and happy life!" To Sir William, then in his seventy-third year, it was happy and timely that fate should bring a change in the sequence of boys. In his own day, his own young family had run rather the other way, with two sons and three daughters. His eldest daughter, Winifred, had given him four grand-daughters but it was all the more pleasant to have a girl through the male line.

Now, with the expectancy over, the tension broken, he could joke fondly and happily with his two "boys" as he always called them, though both brothers had reached their early forties, with Willy flushed and happy over his new parenthood and with Edward, still a bachelor. Their eldest sister, Winifred (Mrs Colegate, later Lady Colegate) was also there, staying for a few days to help support her sister-in-law. Apart from the delighted father, she was perhaps the first to see mother and child, upstairs in the large bright bedroom overlooking the white lawns. With the rich brown bobbed hair of the mother and the pale-spun curly wisps of the sleeping baby, memories long remained of that happy maternal scene.

Meanwhile, the indoor domestic staff had been invited to the dining-room—Miss Robertson, with her wide Scottish smile, Lizzie Keeling, Caroline Hawkins, little Eva Flatters: the cook-housekeeper, the kitchen maid, the two housemaids and the parlour maid. They respectfully sipped to the baby, they found that the champagne tickled, they knew their place and they departed, taking a bottle to offer the gardeners and grooms. A methodical and well-organized man, Captain Worsley telephoned the news to his brother-in-law, Sir Felix Brunner, in London, and then, I think, sat down to write to his absent sisters. Isabel and Victoria had both lived at home until a year or two earlier. Isabel, having vigorously expressed her personality as a first-class woman golfer, sometimes playing for Yorkshire, was sixteen months his junior and was to stage a surprise marriage later that year within a month of her forty-first birthday, while Victoria, an enthusiast of motor trials and Brooklands motor-racing, had married four months previously and had only recently returned from her honeymoon to settle in London.

There was just time to enclose the news of the baby as a message, a timely surprise, on "Vicky's" birthday card, for she would be celebrating her own thirty-third anniversary the very next day, February 23rd. Then, as the last of his paternal duties, Captain Worsley drafted an announcement for *The Times* in nearly the same formal and reticent phrases which he had always used for the birth of his sons.

Hoping to catch the post, he was apparently still engaged in these pleasant chores when the parlour-maid came to the door, hesitantly carrying a potted plant for Mrs Worsley, "sent in from the village, sir". This proved merely the prelude of the local expression of good wishes. The stream of gifts continued until evening and for several days: jars of calves-foot jelly, early flowering bulbs in their pots and dishes, daffodils showing signs of having been purchased in Malton market, and knitted baby garments delayed until they could be threaded with pink ribbon. With their bright messages, they came from the cottages at Brookside, from humble homes in the so-called High Street, from old Miss Corns at the almshouse, from Bingley

Day, the land agent, and his wife, and from the lively Harrisons at
Brinkburn Farm. Such was the regard and esteem in which the
people of Hovingham held the daughter-in-law of their squire. And
the pleasant flow was in full spate when Mr Simpson, the postman,
came beaming across the green, laden with the telegrams of congra-
tulation that resulted from the announcement in *The Times*:

   "*On February 22nd, at Hovingham, Yorks, to Joyce, wife of Captain
W. A. Worsley—a daughter.*"

II

Embowered in a valley of beech and oak, twenty miles north-east of
York, Hovingham Hall has been said by one visitor to resemble a
couched mastiff, gazing vigilantly along the tree-hung slopes, with
the buildings of the village clustered like timorous puppies at its
back. The picture is highly fanciful, for the village is no longer
timorous, and the prospect along the valley is enclosed within a mile
by the hillside rise of Hovingham High Wood. Moreover, the
imaginary mastiff lacks a forepaw, for an intended projecting southern
wing of the mansion was never built. "I built as I could, not as I
would", the Thomas Worsley of the eighteenth century was to sum
up his ten years of prolonged difficulty as an amateur and not always
accurate architect. Yet Thomas Worsley nourished a vision of per-
fection, as did many neighbouring Yorkshire squires of his day, a
vision of idealistic cultivation of the arts and of civilized behaviour
towards one's friends and neighbours, towards tenants and even
horses. Thomas built and founded better than he knew, and today
the old relationship of squire and village is nowhere better preserved than at Hovingham.

   With layer upon layer of time, throughout the village, history
itself has soaked with the sunshine and rain into the gold-grey stones.
Almost adjoining the Hall, just to the north, the village church boasts
a doorway of Saxon work and a rock-firm tower that the Saxons
piled in pious faith course by course towards the sky. A local resident
of an antiquarian turn of mind once enjoyed the freedom of
Hovingham Park to enable him to measure and delve as he wished

into an earthwork a mile west of the house, raised in the dark ages, he asserted, as a defence against Danish invaders from across the North Sea. He found very little evidence but nevertheless claimed with ingenuity that the defenders had lost the day for, a mile or more behind the earthenwork, lies a landmark triumphantly known as Coney Hill, not the hill of the rabbits but a Konig hill, and to the Norsemen the hill of the King.

Everywhere hereabouts are villages still bearing ancient Viking names. The Romans, too, trod the moors and hills, so that when Thomas Worsley first tested the strength of the soil for his massive house, the men found themselves digging up the tessellated paving of a Roman villa; and the road from Malton to Hovingham still indeed follows a Roman line. In this verdant and romantic region, the cadence of past events still murmurs and whispers at every turn, for Hovingham lies at the north-east rim of the Vale of York and, explore as you will, no place better mirrors the Yorkshire story than the Vale—or as some prefer to call it, the Plain—of York, green, far-reaching and uneven, a plain that forms a cynosure of the very history of England.

The City of York itself stands in mid-course between London and Edinburgh, and the plain of York spreads north of the city in the shape like my lady's fan. If you would trace Hovingham upon a map and notice the roads that spread from York like a hand of playing cards, then, with Malton placed ace-high to the east, Hovingham is aptly the jack of hearts.

But there are days of mist and rain when we can imagine the vale of York, fertile and often waterlogged, criss-crossed by no more than the primitive truckways that linked its settlements. The Romans came and, within the walls of York itself, Constantine was proclaimed Caesar and Emperor by the army of Britain. Three centuries later, the Northumbrian King Edwin was baptized here at the behest of his Christian wife from Kent, in a small square wooden church that formed the first foundation of York Minster. Then the Normans destroyed the mother church and built another, and castles, too, across the plain. In 1328, there was already a great timbered house at Hovingham when plump little Philippa of Hainault travelled north to be wed in splendid ceremony to Edward III in York Minster, she a princess aged only fourteen with "eyes black-blue and deep", he a man of fifteen already committed in battle against Robert the Bruce. The child of this very young couple, born two years later, was to be valiantly known as the "Black Prince", England's second Prince of Wales.

One is reminded that the marriage of Philippa and Edward III was the last royal wedding in York Minster until the marriage of Katharine Worsley and the Duke of Kent in 1961. Royal brides, however, were still to traverse the great vale of York. From Sheriff Hutton Castle, not seven miles south of Hovingham, Elizabeth of York was taken to espouse Henry VII after the battle of Bosworth Field, a maid who carried a bridal posy "of red and white roses tied together" to symbolize the end after thirty years of the long War of the Roses.

Incredible as it must appear, in these days of zeal to preserve all that is both old and worthy of the past, I have seen some of the stones of Sheriff Hutton removed to build a modern house. We are all more entoiled in the sequence of past events than we imagine. Across this same plain, Oliver Cromwell's Ironside troops marched to join battle on Marston Moor in the crucial military clash of King and Parliamentarians that finished with the royalists in flight. A few years later, Cromwell's youngest daughter, Mary, also crossed the vale, travelling in splendour to her Yorkshire home, now Newburgh Priory, after her marriage to the rich Viscount Fauconberg. According to the old records, "above one thousand of the gentry" greeted her, all mounted Yorkshire style upon fine horses. It forms a glowing link with our own day that when the present Duke and Duchess of Kent, Prince Edward and his Katherine, were first entertained by Earl Mountbatten at Broadlands, he was able to show them a twelve-sided silver-gilt porringer engraved with the Fauconberg arms, said to have been a wedding gift from the Lord Protector to his daughter.

Nor is this the only heritage of past events, for we shall discover the Romeo-and-Juliet sequel of "two households, both alike in dignity", though not today of ancient grudge, enacted when the Duke of Kent, with his Stuart blood, wished to marry Katharine Worsley, Cromwell's direct descendant. Mary, my lady Fauconberg, was often visited by her elder sister, Frances, to be invariably received "with a great deal of joy and kindness", as Frances wrote to her husband, Sir John Russell. The Fauconbergs had no children of their own, but they treated Viscount Fauconberg's nephew, Thomas Frankland, like a son and, as the years passed, he became doubly a nephew when he fell in love with his beautiful cousin, Elizabeth Russell, the daughter of Frances and grand-daughter of Cromwell, and married her. Thomas Frankland and Elizabeth in turn had a daughter who married into the Worsley family, and their grandson was the Thomas Worsley who built Hovingham Hall.

On the rising rim of the plain of York, in the early years of the eighteenth century, the third Earl of Carlisle had raised the great mansion of Castle Howard, which Thomas Worsley would have seen, pristine and butter-bright, while still a schoolboy, and was evidently stirred to emulate. But perhaps we have lingered too long in the vale of York watching the changing calvacades, the progress and pageantry, the clash and clamour of great events. In the olden times, the plain formed part of the ancient Forest of Galtres, an ancient royal hunting ground known to Henry V. In the sixteenth century, it saw the first-footing of the Merchant Adventurers of York in sending their discoveries and their commerce to the far ends of the world. In the eighteenth century, it saw William Wilberforce wrestling with his conscience in deciding that no men should be slaves, and it watched Laurence Sterne dreamily making his way from cottage to church when he was vicar of Stillington. And in 1961, very much in our own time, the broad plain saw three queens and thirty princes and princesses hastening towards the north-eastern hills to the wedding reception of the Duke and Duchess of Kent at Hovingham Hall.

III

The Worsleys originally came from Lancashire, proudly timing their ancestry from the Norman Conquest, a broad-shouldered deep-chested breed, honest and open but determined to the point of obstinacy, adventurous and with a gallant and enterprising gift for marrying heiresses and making the most of all the apportionments and opportunities that came their way. As early as 1567, in the reign of good Queen Bess, a Worsley acquired Hovingham as the result of a rewarding marriage to a daughter of the rich Sir Thomas Gerard and subsequently laid out a topiary garden as his own memento to posterity. Documents of Charles I's time also show that Worsleys had already been living in the old manor-house for more than eighty years and the intervening centuries have been spent in such placid domesticity that a yew-hedge planted during their early tenure stands to this day, grown both venerable and gigantic.

The old records are incomplete, but in the year 1723 a family of five young orphaned Worsley children were evidently living at Hovingham, two boys and three girls, all of whom had entered the world within the remarkably brief space of five years and by their very number had led to their mother's early demise. That over-prolific lady, indeed, survived her youngest son's baptism by barely a week and the widower father brought up his brood as best he could. It was a credit to him that his three daughters all made remarkably successful marriages; and his fatally born younger son entered the church and lived, by dint of another successful Worsley alliance, to see his children in possession of the far-reaching acres of Ormesby Hall. But our interest lies with the gifted elder son, Thomas, who went away to school at Eton at eight years old and endears himself in perspective by his juvenile drawings of Doric columns and other architectural details carefully delineated in a sketch book when he was still not yet nine.

To the good fortune of his descendants, Thomas Worsley lived at the zenith of that civilized Georgian epoch when the arts and good craftsmanship, so often one and the same, flowered as never before. We can picture him, when at home from school, riding through the young beech woods and over the hills to visit his neighbours at Castle Howard: stocky, thick-limbed and firm-chinned like his fore-fathers, but with the healthy sun-burned skin and crisp curled fair hair of youth.

He would have watched each new building project, every added embellishment, with intense interest. Sir John Vanbrugh, the original designer of Castle Howard, had particularly noted the "spirit of building" that possessed so many of the gentlemen of Yorkshire. But

Vanbrugh had died leaving his "first-born favourite" Castle Howard unfinished, and now gateways and other landscape buildings were rising under the direction of Vanbrugh's collaborator and Sir Christopher Wren's former pupil, Nicholas Hawksmoor. It has been asserted that the third Earl of Carlisle consulted an elder generation of Worsley before he laid a stone at Castle Howard, so considerable was their building knowledge. Hawksmoor said at times that he liked his stonework to look "strong as if from one solid rock", and young Thomas clearly remembered the axiom.

Single-minded, learning on every side, there are still portfolios at Hovingham full of the architectural drawings he collected and stored like a squirrel. Some are of great value, such as Wren's warrant design for St Paul's Cathedral. There are numerous plans for Palladian mansions in the style of Burlington House, decorative designs by William Kent, details of staircases and undercrofts and, more than any other consistent subject, a varied and remarkable collection of designs and drawings for stables, mews and riding schools. These embodied Thomas Worsley's two foremost enthusiasms, architecture and horses. When he planned a house of his own, he first considered the stabling and the needs of his horses, just as a modern young man might think first of his car and his garage.

Thomas had no difficulty in making his way in the world. His grandfather, Sir Thomas Frankland, sometime Postmaster-General, exerted a benevolent influence on his behalf: it was the great age of patronage and no obstacles hindered so acceptable and well-connected a young man in gaining an attachment as equerry to King George III. His nominal duties at Court enabled him to spend a great deal of his London time assimilating royal architecture, from the grand staircase and painted ceilings of Kensington Palace to the sturdy simplicity of the Horse Guards in Whitehall. Whether Thomas Worsley went farther afield, perhaps embracing the grand tour of Italy, has not been established. Yet his neighbour of Castle Howard, the fourth Earl of Carlisle, spent much time in Rome and Thomas may well have travelled abroad with the family. Lord Carlisle acquired and sent home antique statuary by the shipload and there are classic pieces at Hovingham Hall to this day that may have been gifts to Thomas or else trophies of his own vigorous collecting instinct. As early as 1769 a visitor noted the pair of fine Italian bronzes upon his mantelpiece. Much thought and care indeed went into every detail of his home. His father died in 1750, leaving him free at last to demolish the old manor-house; and Thomas, though still unmarried, was completely ready with his building plans, and the masons evidently began work on the Hall within the year.

When the royal guests at Katharine Worsley's wedding drove to Hovingham for the al fresco reception, they approached by the secluded minor road that skirts the southern verge of the park and caught their first glimpse of the mansion from the west, gleaming in the afternoon sun in its dark nest of yews. From this aspect one can glimpse the resemblance to the west wing of Castle Howard, although Hovingham Hall lacks the turrets and domes that give the former such grace. One of the wedding newcomers expected that her car would presently turn into an impressive forecourt or perhaps pass through massive gates down a winding entrance drive, and nothing of the kind in fact occurred. Instead, the royal cars turned through Hovingham village to the eastern side of the house facing its village green, and then passed under a rugged stone archway and vaulted entry and, to their astonishment, the unfamiliar guests were disgorged into a stable, part modern entrance hall, part Georgian riding school.

This surprise was precisely Thomas Worsley's intention. He wished it to be possible, indeed, to ride right through the house into the western garden. In a region celebrated for both horse-breeding and hospitality, he equally purposed to startle and entertain his guests by leading them from the principal reception room on the first floor—now the ballroom—into a gallery from which they could look down at the riding arena and watch the training and feats of equitation of the *manége*.

His friends have unfortunately left us no account of their impressions. A less partial observer, Arthur Young, in making an agricultural tour of England in 1769, considered it odd to find the two best rooms in the house communicating immediately with four or five stables. "Nothing should be condemned because uncommon", he wrote. Nevertheless, he added, "in hot weather, it would be easy to *smell* without being *told*, that the best rooms were built over the apartments of the horses".

In essentials, the amateur architect planned his house on three sides of a square. With access through the rugged arched entrance from the village side, the square itself was roofed to form the riding school. North and South, two wings were to be flung out into the western garden, yet the southern wing was never built and the northern wing, with its palatial staircase, chiefly housed the family apartments. In the one hall interposed between the riding school and the garden, immediately beneath the ballroom, the vaulted ceiling and stout Roman columns are indeed so akin to their fellows in the so-called Grecian Room at Castle Howard that they obviously betray the source of Worsley's inspiration. Though skilled in drawing-board imitation, he nevertheless occasionally overreached himself in practical skill, and his intention of orderly matching windows came to grief in faulty measurements. But these small oddities make Hovingham Hall all the more endearing.

IV

In 1760, the young and good-looking King George III succeeded to the throne of England and, among the political appointments of the new Court, Thomas Worsley was promoted to be Surveyor-General of Works in charge of the maintenance or rebuilding of all the royal palaces. This must have mightily pleased Thomas as a mark of high approval of his architectural prowess, for his predecessors in the post had included none other than Sir Christopher Wren. In the following year Thomas also entered the House of Commons as the member for Orford. One discovers little record of him in Parliament, although he remained in the House for thirteen years. But as the official responsible for the royal palaces, he was probably present at the King's wedding to Queen Charlotte at St James's Palace late in the summer of 1761, an event that affords us a pleasing counter-point to the wedding between his own family and the Royal Family six generations later when Katharine Worsley married George III's direct descendant.

Exerting himself at full pressure in the new reign, Thomas also dutifully launched surveys of the royal apartments at Windsor Castle, Hampton Court, Kensington Palace, St James's and Somerset House, with results set down in a volume still preserved in the Royal Library. A mention of Buckingham Palace is absent, for the King did not purchase the then Buckingham House for his bride until the following year, but the transaction was no sooner completed than Thomas Worsley promptly engaged Robert Adam to prepare a scheme for encasing the brick-built palace in more impressive stone-work.

Adam's proposals were doomed to languish at Hovingham and were never carried to effect. Presumably under the same Surveyor-General, however, he designed doors and ceilings for the new works at Buckingham House and our Thomas himself seems to have made a more lasting contribution by designing the "riding house" that still occupies part of the Royal Mews, solid and strong in Yorkshire style, and still resists the constant tremor of nearby London traffic.

We must mention, too, another sequel. In purchasing Buckingham House for his Queen—some say for £60,000—the King also acquired the murderous and mammoth piece of marble statuary, then thought to depict Cain slaying Abel, which stood at the foot of the magnificent main painted staircase. The young Queen disliked it on sight. She asked very little in the way of structural alterations but clearly decreed that the statue must go. With a more knowledgeable eye, Thomas Worsley no doubt expressed tactful admiration of the work, whereupon his monarch lost no time in telling him that if he liked it, he could have it and should take it away.

It was, in fact, the long-lost group of Samson slaying the Philistine by Giovanni da Bologna, known by sketches in the Uffizi in Florence. Reported missing shortly after one of the Medici princes had presented it to the Duke of Lerma, Prime Minister to Philip II of Spain, it stood in fact in the ducal gardens and was subsequently given by Philip IV to Charles I. As Prince of Wales, in his early twenties, Charles had visited Spain with the Duke of Buckingham to catch a glimpse of the princess Henrietta Maria whom he was expected to wed and instead of a bride, he returned home for the time being with the statue as a royal souvenir, a fierce and cumbersome gift costing £40 of his pocket-money to move from Madrid to the sea. Home in England, the Prince gave it to the Duke of Buckingham, who placed it in the garden of his new London palace, York House, in the Strand. It merely rounds off a chain of coincidence to remember that the present Duchess of Kent, after growing up with the statue at Hovingham Hall, is soon to live in another York House, in St James's . . . and, strangely enough, the statue itself was returned to London shortly before she first met her husband.

When John, Duke of Buckingham, erected Buckingham House, his statuary moved with him to the future royal home and thus passed on purchase to the royal family itself. Readily resourceful in overcoming the immense difficulties of transporting the vast bulk from London to Yorkshire, Thomas Worsley set it up safely in one of the entrance apartments of Hovingham Hall, the room between the riding school and the garden, to become known to his family as the Samson Hall for ever after. The piece was in good company, flanked by the Earl of Carlyle's gifts from Rome and some specimens of Egyptian statuary which were similarly presents from the unperceptive George III to his Surveyor-General. The riding school itself was adorned with paintings in the decorative three-dimensional grisaille style found here and there in Kensington Palace, the work of journeymen Italian painters who found ready employment when visiting England at that time. On his own 1769 tour of inspection, Arthur Young noted the fine marble chimneypieces, the paintings and tapestries and, possibly inspired by Young's visit, Thomas made a catalogue of his pictures the following year. They included works by Rubens, Poussin, Zuccaro, Ostade and others, and they are still at Hovingham.

Thomas Worsley died in 1778, and his grandson was created a baronet in Queen Victoria's Coronation honours sixty years later. His grandson in turn, the third baronet, lived to find himself the grandfather of Katharine Worsley, and it is he whom we have met, as the head of the family, toasting her health on the day she was born. So swift is the ebb and flow, the changing tide of the generations . . .

V

Sir William Henry Worsley, the third "Bart", Katharine's grandfather, once complained, with gentle self-mockery, that he could not

avoid being a true Victorian: he had been born in 1861 and had
married in the year of the Queen's golden jubilee. His bride, a
Scarborough girl of great musical ability, suggests the potential source
of the Duchess of Kent's musical talents and their marriage, a love-
match of two music enthusiasts, was brought about by an innovation
in which the Duchess has similarly an inherited interest. A local
neighbour, Alex Bosville, happened to notice the exceptional acoustics
of the Hovingham riding-school and remarked that it would make a
wonderful auditorium for a concert. The idea was no sooner suggested than put into action. William Worsley had two great passions,
music and cricket, to which he clung with characteristic family
tenacity. Held in 1887, the first concert was a success in every way.
Young Alex Bosville enjoyed himself energetically clashing the cym-
bals in an orchestral overture, and William Henry Worsley immediately fell in love with pretty Mary Chivers Bower and married
her within three months.

The annual Hovingham Music Festival, as it became, developed into
a major music attraction for all Yorkshire. Choristers came from York
Minster; soloists of the calibre of Joachim, the violinist, Plunkett
Greene, the singer, Stanford, the composer and conductor, and others
travelled from London; and the two-day festival was notably renewed
with many well-known instrumentalists for nearly twenty years. The
cricket lawn of the Hall also achieved far more than local celebrity.
The great Ranjitsinhji often played there and the story is still told of a
brilliant though accidental catch when his hand grasped, not the ball,
but the warm pulsating breast of a low-flying swallow.

The "upsurging swell of music and the click of bat against ball"
formed the accompaniment of an exceptionally happy married life.
William and Mary Worsley had two sons and three daughters, whom
we shall meet as the Duchess of Kent's father (the present Sir William
Arthington Worsley), her Uncle Edward and her three aunts,
Winifred, Isabel and Victoria.* The elder son was pressed into concerts
too often during school holidays to share his mother's love of music
with quite the same intensity, but his devotion to cricket became all

---

* Winifred Mary (b. 1888), William Arthington (b. 1890, 4th Bt. and father of
H.R.H. The Duchess of Kent), Edward Marcus (b. 1891), Ethel Isabel (b. 1892) and
Victoria (b. 1900).

the more vigorous. With only fourteen months difference in age, the two boys were both at Eton and subsequently Oxford together, their youth spent in those legendary Edwardian summers that have never yet lost their golden glow. The first world war was not yet a shadow on the limpid horizon. And when the music festivals came to an end, owing to Lady Worsley's ill health, life at Hovingham Hall was never again so tranquil, so sure or so settled.

Around the family the fates now wove circumstances that were tragic and tender and tense and romantic in turn, and strange as any fiction. The eldest girl, Winifred, was also the first to marry in 1912, in a glamorous match with Captain Francis Pemberton of the Life Guards. Her parents celebrated their silver wedding that same year, and ten months later the family suffered the tragic shock of Lady Worsley's death. They had hardly rallied against this heavy blow when, in the following summer, the Archduke Francis Ferdinand was assassinated in Sarajevo and the world took its first precipitate and irretrievable step towards the 1914–18 war. Captain Pemberton's unit was one of the first to cross the Channel and within three months his young wife of two years received a telegram—one of the 800,000 ominous telegrams of that terrible war—to say that he had been killed in action.

"Willy" Worsley was already serving in the Green Howards and his younger brother, "Eddy", had enlisted in the King's Royal Rifles. Both were wounded; "Eddy" indeed was twice wounded and convalesced under medical care at Hovingham Hall, as it happened, for the Hall had become a hospital, while the family remained in one wing and Eddy's elder sisters, Winifred and Isabel, both worked as V.A.D. nurses. The youngest girl, Victoria, could hardly wait for the day when she, too, would pass her V.A.D. exams. There came a grimly anxious time when Captain "Willy", having returned to the Front, was reported missing, and months elapsed before it was known that he had been taken prisoner of war. Happily, also, Mrs Pemberton married again in 1917, when she became Mrs Arthur Colegate, to the joy of young Vicky, her former bridesmaid, who had now become a fully-fledged V.A.D.

Only two other occasions need now engage our interest in the Worsley family chronicles. The first was early in 1919, when all

Hovingham village eagerly awaited Captain Worsley's homecoming. It was a day of days. The family drew lots to decide who should take the car to meet him at Malton, the privilege fell to Victoria and, as they neared Hovingham on returning, they found the road blocked by cheering people. The men of the village meant to celebrate the return in style, and insisted on pulling the car by hand, laughing, cheering and shouting, from the edge of the village to the Hall. The children were released from school to muster, waving union jacks, under the lime trees on the village green, the church bells were rung, and indeed the same merry peals were sounded in welcome nearly six years later when Captain Worsley brought home his bride.

If the return of the squire's son after the war had seen happy rejoicing, his wedding-day was a holiday for Sir William's employees; and there was talk for years of the tenants who went to London—some of the women for the first time in their lives—to see their "Captain Willy" married to Miss Joyce Brunner at St Margaret's, Westminster. "These two, united in holy matrimony" were to be the parents of the Duchess of Kent and it was not least of the felicitous auguries of their wedding that the ceremony was conducted by the then Archbishop of York, Cosmo Gordon Lang, destined to be enthroned as Archbishop of Canterbury four years later and to climax his ecclesiastical career by presiding over the Coronation of King George VI and his Queen.

2 Picking Up Sticks

O had I all that Wealth
Hoptoun's high Mountains fill,
Insured long Life and Health,
And Pleasures at my Will;
I'd promise and fulfil,
That none but bonny she,
The Lass of Peatie's Mill
Should share the same Wi' me.

Old Ballad, 1725
(The May chimes)

I

Tending her floribunda roses beside the old stone dovecot at Hovingham Hall, seated on her pruning trolley on a sunny afternoon, Lady Worsley creates an impression of elderly serenity, her garden gloves and secateurs the accoutrements of a carefree and well-ordered life. Yet the firmer reality is that, when the larger world first heard of her as the mother of the new Duchess of Kent, she felt a sense of gratitude, not only for the thirty-five years of her own married happiness, but of thankfulness also at having seen more than sixty years of fast-changing history and continual family incident.

Born as Joyce Brunner into the intense respectability of South Kensington in the closing years of the last century, she fittingly uttered her first cry amid the parliamentary and domestic ferment that preceded the last general election and last change of government in Queen Victoria's long reign. Her parents, married only a year, had been brought together by sharing the same youthful political convictions. Both were the children of busy Members of Parliament; her father, John Fowler Brunner, was about to offer himself in turn as an election candidate for the Liberal Party and, before she was six

months old, her paternal grandfather would be created a baronet—
Sir John Tomlinson Brunner—in recognition of his service to the
outgoing Liberal government under Lord Rosebery.

Calling at 23 Wetherby Gardens to see the new baby, visitors
mounted the steps of a house that was itself a model of "innovation"
and "reform". Built during the terracotta craze of the eighties, with a
portico of terracotta columns beneath a terracotta architrave, smooth
and red as the chimneypots, the interior seemed in its day equally
unorthodox and modern, with its Axminster carpeting, art-serge
portieres, and the wide white-balustered central staircase—of the kind
beloved by Lutyens—up which the visitors ascended to the baby's
domain.

Number 23 was long since remodelled into flats, like most of the
red brick mansions of the neighbourhood, and few might now
accord it a second glance amid the nearby growing concrete forest of
new hotels. The house next door in the terrace bears a blue L.C.C.
plaque to remind the passer-by that Field Marshal Lord Allenby, the
victor of Gaza and Megiddo, once resided there. No plaque com-
memorates Joyce's father, although in the sum total of quiet human
happiness his contribution was far to outrank those dusty desert
battles.

We have watched the Worsleys in their fertile Yorkshire dales,
landed, contented, proud and protective and, until the present century, shielded from change behind their ancient stone walls and high
yew hedges. Adventurous though domestic, given to impetuous
enthusiasms and more restraining second thoughts, fond in equal
measure of sport and the arts, especially music, reticent and cautious
save among their closest intimates, a residue of all these traits still
moulds the temperament of today's Duchess of Kent. Yet to this one
must add as catalyst the spirit of public service that has run ungrudg-
ing through the Brunners for as long as anyone can measure and, on
this worthy and slightly more foreign side of her personality, we
may trace through four generations the homely, industrious and
sober characteristics of the natives of Zurich canton in Switzerland.

The Brunners indeed establish their family saga no farther back
than a more distant John Brunner, born in 1800 as a son of the
Protestant pastor of the Swiss village of Bulach. Pious and serious-

minded, John Brunner followed his father into the ministry but
decided as a young man that the role of a teacher in England offered
a fuller life in serving his fellows, and by 1835 he had settled in
Liverpool, where he brought an unusual infusion of Manx blood into
the heritage of future royalty by marrying a girl from Balldroma in
the Isle of Man.

In a little-read book of a hundred years ago,* one discovers a
vignette of John Brunner, "practising his profession in a quaint-
looking old house with a detached schoolroom in Netherfield Road,
Everton, a pedagogue to whose fostering care many owe the rudi-
ments of a sound education". In the great age of British industrial
expansion, many of his scholars went to seek their fortunes at the far
ends of the earth, but his two closest pupils, his elder sons, Henry and
John, were destined to find wealth beyond their wildest dreams
almost at their doorstep. By a cruel stroke of fate, their mother died
when they were aged only five and six, and the schoolmaster taught
and brought up his bairns single-handed, just as the father of Thomas
Worsley had done more than a century before.

Both the elder Brunner boys went to work in their early teens as
clerks on Merseyside. With his meticulous copperplate writing and
facility with figures, John Tomlinson, the second son, could add up a
column with a speed that astonished his seniors. Thanks to this
facility, a future of drudgery as a clerk and bookkeeper appeared to
be assured and, at twenty, we find him working for a chemical firm
at Widnes when he met a dark-eyed young lady, a Miss Salome
Davies, whose name suggests that her Welsh blood was combined
with perhaps more exotic strains. They fell in love at first sight and,
after an intimidating interview in Liverpool with her father, it was
agreed that they should marry just as soon as young John Brunner
could better his prospects.

Then everything happened at delectable speed. John audaciously
asked for promotion and was astonished to find himself promptly
appointed a clerical foreman. Within weeks he and Salome were
married—and how delighted old schoolmaster John must have been
to see them both happy! The young couple set up house among the
then orchards and meadows of Farnworth, their windows enjoying a

* Memorials of Liverpool, 1875.

distant prospect of Widnes "with its innumerable chimneys in a background of blue-veiled hills", as a friend poetically wrote of the scene. Three weeks before their first wedding anniversary, their happiness was sealed by the arrival of a baby son, John Fowler Brunner, whom in the fullness of time was destined to be Joyce Brunner's father and the Duchess of Kent's Brunner grandfather.

Salome had made all the baby's things, stitching and embroidering fondly, a layette of love that all the other village women inspected admiringly. John occasionally brought friends home from the works to share an evening meal of cold meat and fresh-baked bread, among them a burly bearded young German chemist named Ludwig Mond, who was living in nearby bachelor lodgings and delighted in relaxing in the Brunners' little home. When Ludwig talked excitedly in his thick guttural accent of recovering sulphur from soda or extracting nitrogen for fertiliser from the very air, Salome must have found the conversation incomprehensible. But he admired her baby devotedly, clucking through his beard at the cradle, and one evening, as if under the spell of a new emotion, he confided his plans of marrying a girl with whom he had already fallen in love back home in Cologne.

Sure enough, later that summer in Germany, he declared his suit and wrote eagerly to the Brunners that he and Frida had married "in the best room . . . beautifully decorated with flowers". There was however a condition attached to his marriage. In giving their consent, Frida's parents had cautiously stipulated that she should not leave for England until a house was ready for her, furnished sufficiently for occupation. John and Salome readily helped the earnest Ludwig furnish the house, even to choosing the best bed and one for the maid.

When Frida at last arrived, they discovered she could speak scarcely a word of English. Unperturbed, they surrounded her with an affectionate welcome. The young bride soon suffered from homesickness, and presently could confide that the kindness of John and Salome had dispersed it. "The Brunners are such dear, simple, good people," she wrote home to her mama in Cologne.

Ludwig and John both painstakingly taught Frida English, perhaps with a slightly Merseyside inflection. When a baby was on the way,

Salome showed her how to make the clothes, as well as providing some indispensables from her own little store. These constant kindnesses between the two women deepened the friendship between the two men. Ludwig, the chemist, was the dreamer, immersed in his inventions and John was firmly the business man, a practical as well as logical head upon his shoulders. Indeed, the first letter he ever wrote to Ludwig Mond began, "Business before pleasure..." and ultimately the two men formed a business partnership, Brunner, Mond—the chemical firm that within twenty years gained breathtaking wealth and within half a century led to the creation of the vast combine of Imperial Chemical Industries.

II

Brunner and Mond, John and Ludwig, the two partners prospered exceedingly—and by 1872, when still in their early thirties, they were looking around for land on which they could build plant of their own for a new process in soda manufacture. With his persuasive financial acumen, John Brunner found investors prepared to put up the then not inconsiderable sum of £5,000 and, with the help of a £12,000 mortgage, the partners were able to purchase the 600 acres of Winnington Park, Cheshire, from Lord Stanley of Alderney. There was no country planning in those days and it was a region already despoiled by salt-pans and chimneys. With the land, moreover, went the empty tumbledown mansion of Winnington Old Hall.

This was all, and more than, the partners wished for their own family accommodation. Beneath the flaking stucco, John Brunner in fact found two buildings, the rugged timberframe of an older Elizabethan black-and-white homestead, and a handsome sandstone wing, added in the eighteenth century. With its octagonal drawing-room and marble chimneypieces, this addition was the work of James Wyatt; and here we have the first fragile royal link of coincidence with the Worsleys, for Wyatt had been one of Thomas Worsley's successors as Surveyor-General to George III.

Ludwig and Frida Mond elected to live in the spacious Georgian

wing, while the Brunners preferred the older and more homely
Tudor part of the house. Salome, alas, died in giving birth to her
fifth child, and the following year, tiring of being a widower, John
married his housekeeper, a most respectable wife on any score, the
daughter of a Dr Wyman of Kettering, of whom Frida none the less
did not approve. This uncomfortable domestic situation not only
perplexed John Brunner but also forced him seriously to question
what he most wished to do with his life. While factory buildings
spread over the fields, he privately preferred to prune his roses. And
as the firm of Brunner Mond prospered and the money poured in,
faster than anyone could spend, he gradually found himself facing
the testing responsibilities of great wealth and, not least, the moral
problem of how money itself should best be used.

Ludwig bought himself a palazzo in Rome, the self-same house
which the artist Zuccaro had built after painting Queen Elizabeth I
and her court in England. He acquired a London mansion and hung
its walls with paintings by Titian and Raphael (now both in the
National Gallery) and his immense philanthropies were to develop
later. John Tomlinson Brunner, on the other hand, discovered a
new public career in turning his energies to the broader field of
education. He devoted his great wealth to building schools and
endowing chairs of economics, physical chemistry and other studies
at Liverpool University. He entered Parliament and served for
twenty-five years with such single purpose that he gradually with-
drew from all his former business interests to devote himself entirely
to public affairs. Winnington Old Hall still stands at the nucleus of
the ICI Winnington Works. But there is no longer anyone there
with Mond or Brunner blood in their veins, and the Duchess of
Kent, it seems, has yet to visit the transformed industrial scene
where her maternal great-grandparents first enjoyed their immense
change of fortune.

We see, too, that her mother, Joyce Brunner, was born, if not
into the lap of luxury, at least into a family that found harmony in
great wealth and liberal ideals. When her grandfather, John
Tomlinson Brunner, was created a baronet in 1895, the doctor's
daughter of whom Frida had so stringently disapproved of course
became Lady Brunner. The distinction of an hereditary title never

* *

came Frida's way, although a group photograph of the 1890's shows the two women seated side by side, clearly good friends.

Joyce Brunner—the Lady Worsley of today—and her younger brother, Felix, now the third baronet, can recollect, like the Worsleys, an Edwardian childhood . . . and theirs, too, was of that sunny and opulent kind that now seems gilded with such remote enchantment. Their nanny was in due time replaced by a governess, the coachman by a chauffeur for Papa's new car and, when Joyce was nine, a strength of extra domestics appeared and they all moved to a larger house, a mansion in Norman Shaw's Dutch style "just around the corner" at 43 Harrington Gardens. Their mother liked to give a regular conversazione, especially for younger Liberals; her children were not necessarily excluded and, unlike the "seen and not heard" small fry of other families, Joyce and Felix were allowed to play their share in intelligent grown-up discussion. When Joyce was ten, a kinsman on her mother's side became Lord Mayor of London, and she was long to remember the sight of her "Uncle Walter", dressed in unaccustomed splendour in his scarlet gown, lace jabot and ruffles, riding in his gilded coach.

At an early age, too, the children knew of the National Trust and the Commons Preservation Society among the good causes their parents supported, and of the founding of garden suburbs in Hampstead and Liverpool. As a girl of twelve, indeed, Joyce was present at the cutting of the first turf of the Hampstead Garden Suburb, a cause so real in terms of effort and emotion that the first tenants later sent her grandfather grateful bouquets from their gardens. A red-haired young man named Winston Churchill occasionally came to tea, and the Asquiths and Stanleys, Morleys and Phipps, were among frequent visitors.

When their father fought his second Parliamentary election in 1906, Joyce and Felix were just old enough to follow the hustings as fervently as the results of the Oxford and Cambridge boat-race. All through her teens the "sensible Miss Brunner" followed the parliamentary news as devotedly as some of her friends studied the tennis championships or the theatre page until, with the Kaiser's war, she threw her youthful energies into Red Cross work, mending and knitting and packing parcels for Serbian refugees. Money meant no more than the small fixed sum which she received for her personal allowance, and it was not until her grandfather died in 1919, leaving unsettled property of nearly £900,000, that Joyce fully learned of her interest in the extensive family trusts and discovered herself already a wealthy young woman in her own right.

She had been bridesmaid to one of her closest friends, Eva Mond (grand-daughter of Ludwig and Frida) back in 1914 when Eva married the young barrister Gerald Isaacs, (son of the then Lord Chief Justice and later second Marquess of Reading). She and Eva were exactly the same age, and Joyce was no doubt chaffed with "You will be next!", but there were signs at about this time that she had begun to consider herself "not the marrying kind". She had flung herself into her father's post-war electioneering campaign and was shaken when he was heavily defeated in the "khaki election". This was no disgrace for Asquith himself lost the seat that he had held for thirty years. A worse blow to her buoyant hopes came, however, in the 1923 election which so heavily stressed the decline of the Liberal Party. Sir John Brunner was defeated at Southport, and at this juncture Joyce was consoled and encouraged by an entirely unexpected new turn in her life in her friendship with Captain "Willy" Worsley.

Eva Mond had introduced her to Arthur Colegate, who was on the staff of Brunner Mond, and whose wife, Winifred, we remember, was Willy's sister. They were an hospitable couple, constantly encouraging Joyce to visit their home at Northwich, a house remembered as being oddly called The Pole. It was up at the Pole, indeed, that she first met Willy, probably during the election campaign. First meetings are seldom as decisive as they appear in fiction, but Captain Worsley was deeply attracted to the intelligent, good-looking and firmly capable girl, and Joyce, too, oddly enough, admired precisely these qualities and more in the handsome, reliable and reassuring man who suddenly filled her whole horizon.

Willy proposed early in the New Year of 1924 and they agreed to marry in London. By a long-standing family tradition the Archbishop of York had officiated at a number of Worsley weddings. The Worsleys, father and sons, had often met Dr Lang at the Yorkshire Club and were indeed old friends: whenever Lang preached in

Hovingham church, he was invariably entertained at Hovingham
Hall, and no great persuasion was needed when the Rector of St
Margaret's, Westminster, invited him to conduct "the marriage of
Captain William Arthington Worsley and Miss Joyce Morgan
Brunner". Londoners, of course, have always delighted in the
pageantry of the parish church of Parliament, in the shadow of Big
Ben. The church bells ring at times as if rejoicing with Big Ben and in
harmony with the bells of Westminster Abbey itself, and for those
interested in personalities the Maytime spectacle of the Worsley
wedding must have been more than usually rewarding.

There was the charming picture of the bride herself, of course, with
her seven bridesmaids and her two diminutive junior pages in their
yellow velvet suits. Among the guests were two ex-Prime Ministers,
with their wives, in the persons of Stanley Baldwin and Herbert
Asquith. Mr Baldwin may have reflected ruefully during the ceremony that it was just a year to the very day since he had been first
appointed Premier, only to suffer inglorious defeat in the House
within eight months, and he would have needed the gift of prophecy
to know that within eighteen months he would be reassuringly
returned to power.

In their side aisle, the Hovingham village folk marvelled at seeing
the great gathering of so many people. The knowledgeable might
have identified the elite of the Yorkshire families: the Normanbys of
Mulgrave Castle, the Gisboroughs of Gisborough Hall, the Becketts of
Kirkdale Manor, the Lawsons of Brough Hall and so on. Members of
Parliament and presidents of good causes—such as Sir Arthur Crosfield
of the National Playing Fields Association—arrived with their ladies,
producing a gleam of top-hats and a flutter of summer millinery. And
then there were Monds and Melchetts, so nearly one and the same, so
difficult for the uninitiated now that Eva Mond was Viscountess
Erleigh and her husband the heir to the Marquess of Reading.

The wedding reception at 43 Harrington Gardens presented that
special enjoyment of the 1920's, a "crush". Champagne glasses
wobbled dangerously in unwary hands; through the hubbub the men
exchanged the not unimportant cricketing news that rain had stopped
Yorkshire play at Leeds—and when the bride and groom left for their
honeymoon in Italy *The Times* correspondent was able to jot a fashion

note, now sweetly period, that the new Mrs Worsley wore "a dark blue alpaca dress with a cerise and blue cloche hat".

III

The newly-weds settled into The Cottage, a pleasant old stone house, just south of the Hall, in Hovingham village. Joyce's sisters-in-law, Isabel and Vicky, continued to look after their father and bachelor brother Eddy at the Hall and welcomed her into the summer blaze of cricketing hospitality. Both had been among her bridesmaids and had introduced her to neighbours and farmers and tenants, and Joyce could not help but enjoy an immediate sense of feeling at home. For the "county" her coming inaugurated a series of welcoming dinner parties, and in the autumn Sir William Worsley repaid the hospitality by, as he said, "reopening the ballroom". This was a masculine decision and Joyce perhaps demurely sat out many of the dances. With the felicity that has often characterized Worsley arrivals, her first child, William Marcus John, was born on April 6th, 1925, a "gift of a son", indeed, on the day after his father's thirty-fifth birthday.

Another son arrived on February 22nd, 1927, and for the first recorded occasion in family annals the boy was named Oliver in recognition of his descent from Oliver Cromwell. Life thus flowed on in placid family event. Both in 1927 and the following year, indeed, Joyce and her one married sister-in-law, Winifred Colegate, were amused to find that they shared pregnancies. Oliver had not long arrived before Winifred had a daughter, and when the Worsleys' third son, John, was born in July, 1928, the Colegates announced another daughter, Victoria Joyce, four weeks later.

Old Sir William Worsley once smilingly took stock of his grand-children in cricketing terms, asserting that with his own two sons there were enough for a family team. It had become a tradition that the county championship eleven, after playing at the Scarborough Festival, should engage in a friendly match at Hovingham, which invariably ended in a family mêlée with nearly everyone joining in. Cricket supplied an extra dimension, and family events and eventful matches tended to be indistinguishable. "The year when Oliver was born, the year we had the New Zealanders at Hovingham," "Willy" Worsley once conjured up the events of 1927. The year of John's birth was also unforgettable in cricketing terms, for this was when Willy himself captained Yorkshire, his eleven including such great names as Sutcliffe and Holmes, Rhodes and Macaulay. His averages in this company were not discreditable. "Yorkshire stands in need of first-rate amateurs," said *Wisden*, and considered that Worsley might prove "a useful batsman . . . his only fault being a propensity to hit out directly he arrives at the wicket". At all events, his team that year advanced in the championship to second honours before he yielded his cap to others.

The away matches had taken Captain Worsley away from home a good deal, and the management of three thousand acres afforded many preoccupations, but the "personal reasons" that he pleaded for this unforeseen retirement lay in his anxiety to be at his wife's side at a difficult time. Joyce and her father had always been especially close to one another and early in the New Year there came a telephone call to tell of his sudden illness. At John's christening party, he had mentioned his optimistic prospects of standing in a by-election at Cheltenham, a town where he had many friends and many links with his boyhood. Instead, events ran darkly against him, and when Sir John Fowler Brunner suffered a final defeat, his health was also at ransom. He was only sixty-three when he died and his son succeeded as Sir Felix Brunner.

Felix, his wife Elizabeth, and Joyce regrouped as families always will. Changes, too, came to Hovingham. The Cottage was becoming too small with three small boys, while Isabel and Victoria were more apt to be drawn away from home by their own concerns, no longer limited to golf and motor-racing. The time had come, in short, for Joyce to take charge at the Hall; the new interest blew away the shadows of bereavement and her father-in-law was the first to encourage her to "change things round a little".

The family had managed for years, for instance, with cumbersome and time-worn chairs in the dining-room, while a perfect Chippendale set was regimented around the walls upstairs in the ballroom. In the drawing-room similarly, stood four painted Adam armchairs which would accord perfectly with the eighteenth century side-tables and ormolu chandelier in the ballroom. Moving the furniture around is indispensable in creating a fresh new home in an old frame and Joyce "rearranged things" with affection, tact and sympathy. Flanking either side of the drawing-room chimneyplace, two oval looking-glasses in heavy gold frames had for years been hung so high that they seldom reflected more than the top of anyone's head. These were replaced with striking effect with two blue-grisaille ovals by Boucher, while the best of the family portraits scattered throughout the house were similarly brought together into the dining-room. "We like to talk about them sometimes," Sir William once said in his joking way, "and they are welcome to eavesdrop."

The paintings in the ballroom also had always been hung one above the other in the crowded old-fashioned way, and their cleaning and subsequent rehanging throughout the house offered Joyce an engrossing interest. Some were displayed to better advantage against the fresh-painted apple-green walls of the adjoining Ionic Room, so-called from its graceful classical pillars. Across the village green from Hovingham Hall, the Worsleys also put in hand the refurbishing of the Worsley Arms Hotel. Here a large and mysterious set of classical decorative paintings had long been lodged in exile. They were, in fact, part of the original decorative paintings of the Hall, perhaps originally from Buckingham House, and have now been restored to the ball-room.

In all these harmonies. Joyce often sought the advice of a Yorkshire neighbour, Mrs Ronald Fife, with whom she had cemented a firm friendship. Known as "Bertie" to her intimates, Margaret Fife had been endowed with the eccentric second name of "Albert" on her birth certificate, perhaps in her father's indignation, unendurable in his mansion in Eaton Square, that she was born a girl and not a boy. "Bertie" had herself gone through all the terrors and disappointments of architectural renovation in restoring Nunnington Hall, which had sunk to the condition of a dilapidated farmhouse, part Tudor, part Victorian, before she took it over and renewed and refurnished it. Apart from her wise and discriminating advice, Joyce and Bertie had much else in common. Both were Londoners, of substantial background, who had found unexpected fulfilment in Yorkshire. If Bertie had no family of her own, in contrast to Mrs Worsley's merry nursery, she made good the difference by adopting children and would discuss with Joyce by the hour the infant problems they presented.

Sorrow in family life is soon followed by sunnier elements. In January, 1931, old Sir William Worsley celebrated his seventieth birthday and heard that same day that Winifred Colegate hoped to present him with another grandchild later that year. Winifred was already in her forties, nearly seven years older than Joyce, and when the new baby proved to be a girl, her fourth, named Isabel Diana, the event intensified Joyce Worsley's own longing for a daughter.

As we know, the hopes were fulfilled, the prayer answered, during the early morning snowstorm on February 22nd, 1933, when Katharine Worsley was born. She arrived with impeccable timing early on her brother Oliver's sixth birthday, enabling her mother to assure her friends radiantly that there was no question of asking for more. The February baby moreover arrived at a time when the Worsley household was as steeped in tender sentiment as the tunes of the longcase clock on the stairs. Captain Worsley's youngest sister, Victoria, had only recently married a London accountant with the romantic and chivalrous name of Arthur Roland King-Farlow, an attachment that seemed to have sprung—and most successfully—from a mutual interest in Brooklands racing cars. And "Vicky's" elder sister, Isabel, also greeted the news of the baby with unfeigned delight. Facing middle-age, she had come to be regarded as irreparably the spinster of the family. But at a party around this time, perhaps Katharine's christening party itself, she seemed irresistibly to be paired with an old family friend, the industrialist, Charles Brotherton . . . and sure enough Isabel and "Charlie" were married five months later. "That makes three wonderful things that have happened," said Joyce, "all within a twelvemonth."

IV

Two small boys, Oliver, aged six, and the four-year-old John, attended the christening of their new sister in Hovingham Church, presumably awed and astonished at the ritual surrounding her. Though only seven, the eldest boy, Marcus, was away at Ludgrove prep school and Captain Worsley thought it better not to disturb his first term. That Sunday afternoon, the weather was dry and warm and the family walked the two or three hundred yards from the Hall to the church, a notable little procession. The scene could not have been more traditional, for the church tower is of Saxon date and the ancient wall seals off the end of the nave as if with a cliff-face of the rugged and solid stone of past events.

At the Saxon font, with her family grouped against this strong and ancient background, the infant received the names of Katharine Lucy Mary, and the Vicar, the Rev. John Jackson, apparently found the baby "well-behaved . . . seraphic", as if ready for any and every ceremonial that life might afford. The sponsors included Katharine's uncle, Sir Felix Brunner, and her Aunt Winifred (Mrs Arthur Colegate) with Margaret Fife as the godmother outside the family and a personable young man, Mr Digby Lawson, aged only twenty-one, whose people had been linked with the Worsleys through three generations of shared local and business interests. They all returned to the Hall for tea, to find the house memorably brilliant with daffodils, and the pleasant family party continued long after Nanny Mist had carried off her little charge to the nursery.

The children's wing lay in the southern part of the house, beyond the Samson Hall and the ballroom above it, and has well been described as a maisonette, as indeed it was, with its own staircase and garden room. Katharine became the centre of this nursery realm when it had already been scuffed by four or five years of small fry, and her environment was mini-masculine. When she cried, it was often because John's square building blocks were found to be causing discomfort in her cot after being presented as a juvenile thank-offering; she inherited teddy-bears, a variety of soft balls and a model farmyard and ventured her first steps across a floor already commandeered by toy soldiers.

An old box of snapshots still show the child, building castles in her sand-pit in a corner of the rose-garden, and struggling to pull a wooden model of an open-decked London omnibus which, one suspects, had originally been carpentered by her Uncle Edward as a labour of love for young Marcus. In other pictures, she sits concentrating on a toy in an old-fashioned pram that had clearly seen stalwart service with her brothers. Smiling and absorbed, she plays with the cups and saucers of her doll's tea-set and, shyly posed, with her spun-gold hair and rounded cheeks, the little Katharine is already discernibly the woman of today. Captain Worsley liked to introduce her to his cricket friends, saying proudly, "My young daughter!", but the resemblance was always evident.

Katharine can scarcely remember her grandfather, who died in 1936 in his seventy-fifth year. But the old man liked to stroll with her across his beloved lawns, here indicating a rabbit-scratch to be pressed down or encouraging her to stamp out with her tiny feet some other small imperfection. In his last autumn, when the gales whipped a lavish ransom from the trees, it became her special task to pick up twigs and she raced here and there, gathering her harvest of sticks with lively enthusiasm. In summer, her joy was to wield a miniature toy watering can among the flower-beds, but when aged four or five, bonneted and in wellingtons, ready for any weather, Nanny Mist had only to suggest "Let's pick up the sticks" to set her little charge energetically trotting back and forth with her burdens until teatime.

All three of her brothers were now at Ludgrove prep school. (Marcus, indeed, went on to Eton when his sister was still only five.) Hereditary titles are frequently bewildering with their ever-changing names, but Katherine's parents were now of course Sir William and Lady Worsley, and Joyce perhaps could not suppress her surprise when the staff first meticulously addressed her as "My lady". With the boys all away at school, Katharine might have been regarded as a lonely child, and an early photograph shows her as a tiny bridesmaid at a Yorkshire wedding, over-solemn and anxious. Yet the house could hardly contain her exuberance—or that of her brothers—when they were all home for holidays. There were summer months, too, spent at Selsey with her Brunner cousins, Uncle Felix's sons, including Timothy, Dan and Hugo who were nearly her own age. And then there were the visits of her Colegate cousins, especially the two youngest, Victoria Joyce and Isabel Diana.

One recognizes their names, carried down in the old family context. Aunt Isabel, it must be mentioned, duly married her Charles Brotherton only to die tragically on the eve of her wedding anniversary two years later. It was a resource in Charles's strength of character, part of the secret of his success in business, that he quickly sidestepped the heaviest blows and, with his yearning for a son or daughter still unsatisfied, his undiminished optimism was not long in returning. The Worsleys were not surprised some eighteen months later to be invited to another wedding, in fact his third. His new wife became affectionately known to the family as "Muffy" but in fact she muffed nothing. And one weekend at Hovingham early in the New Year of 1939 Charlie's jauntiness knew no bounds: he could not contain his delight that a baby was on the way.

"I'm going to give her the finest pearl necklace money can buy " he announced. "I'm going to give her a string of the finest pearls in the world." His wife presented him with an heiress (and later with an heir) and, with all the world as an emporium for his gift, the changes of coincidence were rung curiously close to the Worsleys with a significance unrealized at the time. For Charles Brotherton discovered a superb string of pearls that had belonged to a Czarina of Russia and he privately purchased the necklace from none other than Princess Nicholas, the mother of Princess Marina, the then Duchess of Kent.

In the same year, too, by a chance no less strange, the Worsleys also established their first link with the Duke of Kent. Back in 1934, they had been delighted, like everyone else in England to hear of the engagement of the youngest and most handsome of King George V's sons, Prince George, with the beautiful Princess Marina of Greece. Katharine was just twenty months old when, during the wedding preparations, Prince George was created Duke of Kent, reviving the royal title formerly held by the father of Queen Victoria. It is tempting to picture Nanny Mist studying the pictures in the newspapers, unaware that a future Duchess of Kent played at her feet.

Lady Worsley moreover followed the news with more intimate attention, for the marriage ceremony was to be conducted by the Archbishop, *her* Archbishop, the self-same Cosmo Gordon Lang who had conducted her own marriage service as Archbishop of York and was now to conduct his first royal wedding as Archbishop of Canterbury. The marriage ceremony was the first ever to be broadcast and Lady Worsley listened with tangible emotion as she heard the same familiar voice pronouncing the words that she herself had heard as a bride ten years before.

It was all the more pleasant to read almost a year later of the birth of

Prince Edward (on October 9th, 1935) and then, within another year, the birth of Princess Alexandra on Christmas Day, 1936. Midway between these events, Nanny Mist must also have read with closer domestic interest of the birth of a daughter to Elaine Brunner, formerly Howlett, the only daughter of the redoubtable Mr Howlett, King George V's valet. Elaine was the wife of Lady Worsley's first cousin, and Nanny Mist's starched apron surely rustled with excitement when she read that Queen Mary was a sponsor to this baby of Brunner blood at the christening at the Chapel Royal, St James's.

But our concern is with Katharine, and in 1939 the spark of interest was brightly rekindled when the Duke of Kent visited Yorkshire for a three-day tour of social service activities. On Wednesday, June 28th, he lunched with the Lord Mayor of York and then visited Hovingham in the afternoon to open the new village hall. It was to have been a flying visit sandwiched between inspections at Thirly and Easingwold, but Sir William suggested an adjournment to his house for refreshment and, while the Duke of Kent was admiring the cricket-pitch, the little figure of Katharine came down the path. "My daughter," said Sir William, with his usual pride and Katharine extended her chubby hand. She was accustomed to tall blue-eyed men gazing down at her, and to the hazards of their strong fingers. This one did not harm her. As was his way with children he admired, the Duke swept her to shoulder height from off the ground to hold her and talk to her, as he so often did with his own, Edward and Alexandra. And now Katharine . . .

The incident was trivial, a mere nothing. It merely embroiders the tale to learn that within forty-eight hours the Duke's next public engagement, was to fly with his wife to a royal wedding in Italy. And it remains an extraordinary fact that, for the past thirty years, a photograph of the late Duke of Kent has hung in the village hall at Hovingham, the only royal portrait on public view anywhere in the village and the only royal portrait indeed to challenge the Cromwellian portraits that hang in Hovingham Hall.

3 A Wartime Childhood

We follow brave Hannibal and Scipio
Who were great warriors all the world does know
Hannibal Conquered o'er the Alps of Italy
Where mighty Eugene march'd, fought and set us free

A Song to the March in Scipio
(The April chimes)

I

The child Katharine was six-and-a-half when war broke out in 1939 and twelve years old when hostilities ended. No one could fit more closely into the definition of a wartime childhood, sheltered and yet threaded into the texture of resolve and effort of a Yorkshire village. Her father rejoined his old regiment, the Green Howards, and his appearance in battle-dress must have seemed an inexplicable event linked with a visit from friendly Mr Day, the air-raid warden, who came over from his home at nearby Pasture House to fit her with a gas-mask as if it were an amusing new game. Suddenly there were groups of strange children wandering about the village, talking together in thick Durham accents incomprehensible to the puzzled little girl from the Hall. They attended Sunday School, eyed with uncertainty by the regulars, until a companionable bag of sweets was passed along the rows. These perplexing visitants were the local quota of sixty evacuees from Sunderland, but Katharine could well understand that they had come to Hovingham, as her mother explained, because it was safe for children and was a nice place to be, in wartime.

Into Katherine's life had also come a governess, Miss Evelyn Brockhurst, sparse, pale and elderly. When the wavering moan of the air-raid siren sounded an alert, the household gathered around the stout Roman columns in the Tapestry Hall, which was thought even safer than the adjoining Samson Hall. The window shutters were half-closed to lessen the supposed risk of blast and Miss Brockhurst engaged her small pupil in engrossing games of snakes-and-ladders at the long elm table, though before long the alerts were ignored, for no one could believe in danger in the calm and autumn-tinted countryside. Soldiers and army hutments appeared as if by after-thought in the park; there were children's parties for the evacuees; and when Katharine's three brothers came home from school for Christmas, the festivities that first year were bright and gay as ever.

It took time for the idea and practice of war to seep in, and it was seven months or more before war dwelt in the village and in the house like a grim stranger. Katharine first learned to use a needle and thread encouraged by her mother's Women's Institute ladies, who met for sewing parties in the Tapestry Hall, watched stitch by stitch, as in allegory, by martial figures on the tapestries that had once graced Imperial walls in Vienna. Though woven in Austria, a Roman soldier appeared to be a particular friend, consulting the auguries before marching into battle. Katharine, too, is remembered with Colegate cousins, evacuees and small friends presiding at a junior-sized gateleg table, perhaps for the unrationed cake of her seventh birthday. Later on, in that sunshine summer of the Battle of Britain, the cricket lawn was again her anxious concern and she solemnly paced the greensward looking for shrapnel splinters—once Miss Brockhurst knew them to be harmless. Jagged silvery pebbles, they were collected triumphantly in a cardboard box and ultimately disappeared in one of the Hovingham salvage drives. When the soldiers played cricket, Katharine expertly marshalled the number-signs for the score-board or occasionally went in to bat, wielding her own miniature cricket-bat, a fair and sturdy little mascot, not with-out skill.

If Princess Elizabeth's broadcast to the children of Britain produced little impression, she stoically contributed a regular penny from her pocket-money to Mrs Stonehouse's 1d a week Red Cross fund. Tanks and battleships shared her grave scrutiny with ponies and railway engines in the pages of her *Children's Newspaper*, and she gazed wide-eyed at the armoured vehicles that presently lumbered past Hovingham green, knowing that they had much to do with the downfall of "that horrid Hitler" who capered so comically in the newspaper cartoons. After all, it helped, as Miss Brockhurst realized, to have been brought up in daily view of Samson slaying the Philistine, a clear example that the wicked had to be punished and would be brought low.

Her Aunt Vicky came one weekend, strange and seeming taller in A.T.S. uniform. Katharine fingered the buttons, made no sense from the initials of the Auxiliary Territorial Service and enquired, "Shall I wear uniform when I grow up?" It was to be hoped that the war would not last that long, and how should Vicky foresee that her niece would indeed one day wear uniform—as chief of the A.T.S. and Controller Commandant of the Women's Royal Army Corps?

Seaside visits to Scarborough belonged to the past, but Kathie's youngest Colegate cousin, Diana, was one of her constant companions that summer and the two little girls happily patted out sandpies at the wooden-framed sand-pit in the garden. The phase of the Battle of Britain passed into the civilian endurance of the Blitz and a "child's shelter" arrived, a cage of sturdy wire mesh, into which Katharine crawled only once or twice before her brothers discovered its usefulness to support their table-tennis board when trestles were needed elsewhere. Katharine's first experiments with music at about this time were quite illicit: fingering the piano in the ballroom occasionally when she passed through from the nursery, forbidden fruit that tasted all the sweeter. A lady began coming in from Malton to give her twice-weekly piano lessons, her music teacher and a Pony Club riding instructor often arriving on the same local bus.

Yet it was when Oliver and John were home that the little girl of the Hall was happiest, noisiest and most venturesome. "Come up, Kate!" Oliver would cry, whirling her perilously to the front of his saddle, and within a year or two all three went riding together, the girl between the two schoolboys, trotting up to the High Wood to see the foresters or to visit the Illingworths, a neighbouring family who then lived at Wool Knoll. John's acquaintance was always wider and more audacious: he knew woodsmen and soldiers, land-girls and searchlight crews and could always charm cakes and fizzy lemonade out of Margy, Mary and Mabel, the trio who ran the Naafi canteen in Hovingham Park. "We don't serve civilians", Margy Rogers would say, reproachfully, but regarded them fondly nevertheless as club members. Inevitably, Marcus, the eldest boy, seldom shared these expeditions, in his seventeenth year, almost a man. It was Oliver who aroused Katharine to a pitch of fun and excitement, putting his pony at the practice fences, back and forth, while she obediently raised the rails higher and higher. And it was John who foresaw and devised special treats for her delectation. "Can't she stay up tonight?" he would beg, "to see the searchlights?"

They came as a surprise, indeed, the distant white pencils sweeping the western night sky, the closest one casting a false flickering moonlight on the house. She had been unaware in her own secure evenings, of the display beyond the thick black-out curtains. There were nights when enemy bombers throbbed overhead and the air presently vibrated like a string to the guns of York twenty miles distant. "One of theirs? One of ours?" the grown-ups might question. And there were nights when the remote crackle and bark of the anti-aircraft batteries, the deeper crump of the bombs, drowsed Katharine to sleep, a distant familiar trembling of sound far less frightening than a summer thunder-storm.

II

As a child, Katharine was always a popular bridesmaid, Saxon-blonde, so pretty and self-assured. Her family has lost count of the number of times—was it four or five?—when she processed up the aisle, posy burdened, at the weddings of neighbours or cousins. Yet one wedding was to bring rich new threads of affection to her life although, to her disappointment, she did not attend it. Her Uncle "Eddy", her father's only brother, had seemed an incorrigible bachelor, and suddenly one day, early in 1941, when nearly fifty, he startled the family and delighted his eight-year-old niece by announcing his intention of getting married. His intended bride, the daughter of an underwriter at Lloyd's, was half his age but any headshaking was rapidly stilled by the charming impression that his fiancée, Joyce Beer, instantly made at Hovingham, a pleasant brunette, dark-eyed, beautiful, and yet as diffident as the Worsleys themselves. She and Katharine took to one another at once.

"This is your new Aunt Joyce."

"But my mummy's name is Joyce."

There was some such exchange, embracing the discovery that both would be Joyce Worsley, like a poetic enchantment in a fairytale, and Katharine's response was one of immediate and total dedication. The wedding took place in June, less than a week before her Uncle Edward's epochal birthday, at Holy Trinity, Kensington. But this was also during the London blitz and Katharine, to her chagrin, remained in the school-room at Hovingham Hall, where her governess instructed her small class of cousins and two or three evacuees. Her reward in due course was a specially large piece of wedding cake, magically mixed with wartime ingredients, and shared for the nursery tea. The wedding itself was a notable family gathering. Marcus, Oliver and John came up from Eton, where all three brothers were in Mr W. N. Roe's house that term, an unusual if not unique family representation. And then there was Aunt Winifred with some of her family, and Aunt Vicky rushed from her A.T.S. base, conveniently near in London.

The new Joyce Worsley—Aunt Joyce, as she became—could now be dubbed Katharine's favourite aunt, just as she was undeniably the youngest, destined to become an important influence in Katharine's early life and, indeed, to become a discreet essential accessory in the royal romance of twenty years later. Her quick affection for her niece must have smoothed her own southern sense of strangeness in living in Yorkshire. Her husband was serving in the King's Royal Rifles and she moved into Cawton Hall, a mile away at a corner of the Hovingham estate, to establish a home under wartime difficulties. On tuition riding expeditions, Katharine would suggest "going to help Aunt Joyce", and adults noted the new flavour of "strength-and-honey" in the little girl's character, like a blossom opening to morning sun.

She helped her mother hull the strawberries for jam, clapping her hands and dancing with excitement when a sample pot of Lady Worsley's "plum and strawberry" gained a first at the summer produce show. When aged nine, she bestowed a share of her affection upon a rabbit which she groomed and cosseted and entered in the local Rabbit Fanciers Show and duly won a first prize in the "juvenile pure breeding" class, her first accolade for individual effort. The youngest volunteer at a Christmas Fair in the Riding School (which seemed to gain capital initials at about this time), she helped at the tea stall, wildly dashing off to help wash up when the stall ran directly short of tea-cups. She was, people said, "her mother all over again", and Lady Worsley was president of the local Women's Institute, founder and president of a children's home in York, deeply involved in the county W.V.S. and the first woman in England to organize a Parish Produce Association for the efficient production and business-like marketing of home foodstuffs.

A white-painted notice-board appeared near the village hall with the announcement, "BY WORKING TOGETHER WE HAVE ACCOMPLISHED THIS WAR WORK" and there followed an impressive list of the foodstuffs produced, the money raised for the Red Cross and other causes, the tonnage of waste-paper collected, the yield from salvaged metal scrap in terms of bullets and guns, and so on. Katharine did her share in packaging gifts "for the bombed areas of Finsbury" and in "collecting books for hospitals and the Forces". Old Mr Suffield, Hovingham's oldest inhabitant, reputed to be over ninety, brought out some ragged volumes he had bought as a young man, and Katharine without any prompting took him a jar of apple-jelly in return. Spending her monthly sweet ration, her "points coupons" at the little general store, the story is told that she hesitated between liquorice allsorts and longer-lasting gum-drops. Another child came in and asked for a chocolate bar but had not enough points. "Oh, please, cut some from my page, Mrs Bell," pleaded Katharine, "I have five points to spare." Village people still vividly remembered such things twenty years later.

Then there was the cropping campaign for rose-hips one summer when the Produce Association was buying rose-hips from collectors at 2d per pound, meticulously weighed out on the scales. Katharine snipped and picked the hips assiduously to increase her pocket-money only to donate her gains impulsively to a collecting-box that went round when a charity group were being entertained to tea in the Riding School. She is remembered, aged about nine, presiding over a lucky dip during a children's sports day on the cricket field, advising the rich and elderly where to dip and laughing mischievously when they lost their pennies. She was an active usherette when the village folk came to watch a folk-dancing display on the lawns, attentively leading people who wore glasses to front seats "because you have to see better". The war news does not affect a child but, when a young farm lad of her acquaintance was killed during tree-felling, the tragedy had to be concealed from the soft-hearted Katharine. When an old lady was ill in bed, she took her some magazines. "How long will Mrs Harrison take to read them? Because I will bring her some more, and take these to others." If some of the tales have been gilded with passing time, they are none the less representative.

Other children were perhaps less noticed. She was the squire's daughter—the squire's only daughter—in a village that remained curiously feudal in character. The relationship of Hall and hamlet had scarcely changed in the 150 years since Miss Mitford wrote *Our Village*, another village where "in every condition of life goodness and happiness may be found by those who seek them". As a son of the Hall, when home from school, Oliver presented the whist drive prizes in the new village hall, and his young sister helped hang the coloured lights for a dance for the land-girls and army gunners and locals. The Women's Institute eventually held their make-do-and-mend classes at the village hall also, and once a month the W.I. Secretary, Mrs Hynes, the schoolmaster, the vicar, local farmers and others would walk through the Riding School and skirt the Samson Hall to the Tapestry Hall, for the committee meeting of the Parish Produce Association with Lady Worsley presiding.

There were afternoon occasions—planning a "shop" for a prisoners-of-war fund—when Katharine would hear the scrape of chairs and benches indicating the end of a meeting and run lightly down the stairway from the privacy of the house to stroll back with the guests across the quadrangle of the Riding School and bid them goodbye. "My young deputy," Lady Worsley would call her fondly. The deputy was never afraid to ask questions and gained more knowledge of local people within minutes than all the household during the rest of the day. She seemed to know of village weddings before anyone else, and followed with partisan interest the drama of an evacuee boy who refused to return home and hired himself out instead to a local farmer. The village would like to have known more of an occasion when Archbishop Garbett preached in Hovingham church and afterwards lunched with the vicar at the Hall, but for such home occasions Katharine "simply absorbed gossip like a cotton-wool pad without ever breaching discretion". Only Aunt Joyce, it seems, was ever trusted with confidences. In the immutable course of events, her father accepted Army retirement and became a magistrate at Malton court, as well as colonel of the Army Cadet Corps. If, at the family lunch-table, he occasionally wished to discuss the morning's cases, he knew that his wife and daughter "would take nothing farther".

"Come home and have a cup of tea with me," one of the Hovingham ladies might invite "young Kate". "Come and see the wonderful doll my little girl has had from her father in Libya." Friendly and safe, Katharine trod the familiar path across the green, under the towering lime trees, perhaps to the Bells in the little post office and general store, perhaps to the cluster of brookside cottages beyond the church, or on an errand to one of the larger houses in Park Street. That familiar path! "A little world . . . close-packed and in-sulated," like Miss Mitford's Cranford, where Katharine knew every-one, and yet it was still unthinkable in those days that she should go to the village school.

In 1943, when she was ten years old, the problem of her education grew more pressing. Lady Worsley was a delegate that July to the W.I. conference in London and took her daughter with her, though not, unhappily for biographical tidiness, to the Albert Hall, where the delegates were addressed by the Queen, the present Queen Mother, Katharine's future Aunt Elizabeth. Light as the Bailey bridges that the Allies flung across the river of Italy later that year, this London visit and another stay with her Aunt Elizabeth and Uncle Felix were to link the phase of the nursery schoolroom with the budding schoolgirl. For it had been successfully arranged that Katharine should go to Queen Margaret's School at Castle Howard in the autumn.

III

At this distance of time it might seem like going to school in a palace, although a palace stripped and dismantled, and terribly ravaged by fire. "I have seen gigantic palaces before, but never a sublime one", wrote Horace Walpole, with his infectious enthusiasm, after visiting Castle Howard, and sightseers have flocked there ever since, achieving in our own day the astonishing total of 100,000 visitors a year. This ranks second only to Harewood in the gate statistics of northern stately homes, and the discriminating might rank the soaring splendours of Vanbrugh's masterpiece first in esteem. Yet, for Katharine, until the age of ten, Castle Howard was no more than a larger house of the neighbourhood, one of the accustomed objectives of rides with her brothers through their beloved woods, the friendly backdrop of birthday parties with Howard children ... and not least with her near-namesake, Catherine, only two years older then herself.

The Howard family lived during the war in the east gate-house, while the mansion itself was occupied by Queen Margaret's School, an "amazingly happy" sanctuary, as the head-mistress reported. Bomb damage had deprived the school of its original Scarborough home and, walking through the district early in the war, the Yorkshire writer, Oswald Harland, was under the impression that the Howards "had gone from Castle Howard ... the place is a boarding school for girls." Peering through the glass of the main door, he saw "ponderous marble and the heavy gilding, the monumental solidity, the great staircase, the gallery, the dome, the vast fireplace ..." Reconnoitring the exterior, he discovered the gymnasium with "wall-bars, vaulting-horses, scales, ropes and all—but the girls were on holiday and the place was empty." Yet had he arrived a day or two or even minutes earlier, he might well have found it echoing to the high-spirited whoops of the combined Howard and Worsley youth, for it had been the Howard family gym and out of term-time they still colonised it as their own.

He might have seen Katharine clinging perilously to a rope, triumphantly crying "Look at me! Look at me!" or perhaps John and Oliver swaying frantically on a rope ladder. So memorable was the fun that, thirty years later, John had a rope-ladder hung from a beam for his own children in Ontario—and his sister, as a visiting royalty, forsook adult dignity and reaffirmed lasting popularity with the small fry by clambering up it rung by rung.

Equally, if Mr Harland had delayed his exploration of the neighbourhood by three months, he could well have witnessed the lurid catastrophe of the Castle Howard fire. Every child has probably day-dreamed of being sent home because the school had burned down, but the Duchess of Kent has friends of her schooldays to whom this really happened. Although the fire occurred in November, 1940, and Katharine was not a pupil at Queen Margaret's until the autumn of 1943, it was the first news event with which she nevertheless felt closely concerned. For weeks everyone in Hovingham talked of little else, with much head-shaking, and when her brothers came home for Christmas, she rode with them to view the damage, catching the infection of their excitement and dismay.

Not that there was a great deal for her to remember, save the acrid smell of blistered stone, the dark distortion of the burned-out dome and the empty south front windows, sharing the vacant light of roofless rooms. Nothing indeed, as Miss Brockhurst had said, for a small girl to see. And yet, at the gate-house, Katharine also gained from the grown-ups the sense of relief, the hint of a blessing disguised, that it had not been "due to Hitler".

In the darkness, on the night of the fire, the disaster fed on itself in, perhaps, a chapter of accidents and misunderstanding. A teacher remembers being aroused by a colleague with the words, "Come quickly! the office is on fire. Bring a wet towel—there's a lot of smoke!" But it was unimaginably worse than that. The staff had fire-drilled a score of times, and now those "on fire extinguishers" ran coughing through the smoke to find the walls and furnishing of the office in flames to the ceiling and others "on hose duty" realized from the gusts of intense heat, the sparkle and glare, that all three rooms of the south-east corner—the once—lovely drawing-room, the glorious High Saloon, the so-called Queen's Room—were fiercely ablaze. Another group were bringing out the children and trooping them safely, mainly clad in blankets, across the northern courtyard to refuge in the far west wing of the house.

Later, the children's clothing was retrieved and, later still, a working party of older girls carried their mattresses away from the chief remaining hazard of being soaked by water. There were hours of great alarm and yet not a moment when the children were at risk. In the lurid half-light, the headmistress went alone through the dormitories, running her hands over each bed to make sure no child was left behind. Yet, in the excitement, one group thought that the fire brigade had been summoned when they had not been, and during this natural confusion precious time was lost.

The fire stories were like personal bomb stories, told and retold afterwards, how one group of the staff played their hoses on hot and steaming walls to save the Canalettos, how the sixth form helped to rescue the more valuable books and pictures from the main corridor, how the men of the local searchlight unit performed prodigious feats of strength carrying out old and heavy furniture and then had to race back to their posts when an air-raid warning sounded, "a rather upsetting occurrence", as one teacher noted, drily, conscious that the house was now a fiery beacon visible for miles. An east wind fanned the flames, the weeds and low level of water in the south lake handicapped the fire brigades, and at last the dome itself collapsed, crashing seventy feet in a mighty gust of sparks into the hall.

Amid all the images of flame and terror, a household worker vividly recollects "the sight of water, gallons of water, cascading down the stairs, the basement passages all awash". But the fall of the dome signalled the crescendo of the fire and the turning-point of its control. In the west wing, breakfast had by then been served on time, with a fifth-former reporting the deep battle between her "hunger for porridge and the wish to watch". And more splendid still, while the wreckage of half the rooms of the south front steamed and smouldered, the kitchen staff as their supreme triumph served the school a hot lunch.

That night, before parents could fetch them away, many of the girls were sheltered in houses throughout the district, including Hovingham Hall. Yet within a few months everything at Castle Howard was so normal that Katharine, as a neighbourhood guest, was able to watch a school performance of Twelfth Night, set against the north facade of the house, and she is remembered "sitting stock still for once" at a piano recital by Maurice Cole. Small events retreat into obscure recollection, but when Katharine attended Queen Margaret's as a day girl in 1943 she fitted into the new dimension of school life at Castle Howard snugly as into a glove.

IV

Among the visitors to Castle Howard, Easter to October, there are frequently former Queen Margaret's girls, Old Margaretians, who "remember it when . . ." The pattern of the mansion admirably lent itself to division into two school houses, "The Hall", sleeping in the east wing, and "School House", to the west. The visitors, whether "Hall" or "School" recollect when the Tapestry Room, the Music Room and the Orleans Room on the south front were class-rooms, each with its blackboard and platoon of desks. They recall Lady Georgina's gold-and-yellow bedroom as one of the cosier dormitories, filled with iron bedsteads, and at times they fail to identify even the windows of their own "dorms", that bedroom or this dressing-room—it all looks so different now! Mothers or aunts, they lead their own puzzled children up the Grand staircase, past the Roman portrait busts, "but these weren't here then". And if they should pause in perplexity before that remarkable relic, the altar of the temple of Delphi, they find the ancient oracle mute to the essence of their own riddles: so long ago since their school-days, so short a time.

The senior girls dined at small tables ranged down the so-called Antique Passage, where Ceres, goddess of plenty, presides today, although then fittingly banished with the other statuary to the cellars, unable to preside over whalemeat and the canned meat called spam. Wartime Margaretians recollect when grass sprouted from the charred timbers that littered the paving of the Hall, deep beneath the skeletal ruin of the dome. And, curiously, nearly everyone who was at school with the Duchess of Kent appears to remember her, a lively high-spirited little figure, slightly plump, flaxen fair, her hair worn in those days in madonna plaits . . . but, above all perhaps, memorable because she sometimes rode to school on a horse.

Katharine Worsley was one of thirty new girls that term, yet evidently she was one of the very few day pupils, and at one time the only day girl, accordingly envied as such by many although scorned by a few. Being a "droopy Day" was an unsought and undesired distinction that she at first tried to minimize, begging when brought to school by car to be dropped at the Obelisk on the main road, nearly half a mile from the house. Petrol rationing caused Hovingham folk to pool their journeying, so that she sometimes travelled with her father on his way to York, or occasionally with Dr Learmont or the parson or the Dawnays from Malton, always polite in thanks before running away down the entrance drive. The first assembly of term was held at the southern end of the Long Gallery, where the sumptuous Van Dyck and Lely portraits still hung undisturbed and so, on her first debut in the wider world, she came under the token gaze of Queen Henrietta Maria, whose descendant she was to wed within eighteen years and within a distance of rather less than eighteen miles.

Nor was this the only circumstance strangely caught up in the tapestry. On six days a week, the school—seniors and juniors alike— gathered for morning prayers in the Howard family chapel, drawing another curious link in the threads of time. As this book goes to press, the Duke and Duchess of Kent plan to move into York House, St James's, as their new London home and may adopt the Chapel Royal, St James's, as their accustomed place of worship. Attending a service there for the first time, for a friend's wedding not long ago, the Duchess was stirred suddenly by the *deja vu* sense of familiarity, of an irresistible reminder of her schooldays. The Chapel Royal had only just been refurbished, with the rich and intricate Holbein ceiling cleaned and newly illuminated by cornice lighting—and the only copy of that Holbein ceiling is that of the chapel of Castle Howard.

Susceptible to such chords of atmosphere, the Duchess at Queen Margaret's was attached to "School House" and cast, as one senior says, into the nether regions of the junior school, around the so-called Grecian Hall (the present-day restaurant and cafeteria) a storey below the principal floor of the building. So the ten-year-old Katharine moves in her own dimension of time among the tea-urns of today; but with its stout stone pillars and vaulted ceilings this was precisely the region that most resembled the familiar Samson and Tapestry

Halls at Hovingham. In this more domestic atmosphere, she spent her first term in form IVB, quickly promoted after Christmas to Form IVA, just along the corridor. She had her first school piano lesson in one of the rooms somewhere below the stylish Reynolds portraits of the Tapestry Room and won a "credit" in her first year in the elementary piano examination. She was found notably fond of music, painting and drawing, and entered in one school record as "very musical and artistic generally".

"Quite a good worker," her form mistress assessed her, "though I do remember she did not like Latin very much. She thoroughly enjoyed games and gymnastics and was good at them and she was particularly good at cricket. She was a delightful child to have in a class; very merry and bright and ready for a bit of mischief." The surviving school magazines cast some light on her activities. What did the young Katharine make, one wonders, of the Sixth Form performance of *St Joan*, or what dreams were stirred by a piano recital by Kathleen Long? In the New Year, the junior school's production of *Peter Pan* serves to indicate why the Duchess of Kent once discovered that she shared an unexpected familiarity with the text with Lord Snowdon, who once played Peter in a childhood family production. And when the Duke and Duchess of Kent lived in Hong-Kong were there perhaps memories of the school production of *The Mikado*, of the bookcases in the Long Gallery framed in cherry-trees, a glade down which advanced the "three little girls from school"?

A month after Katharine's eleventh birthday, there occurred a most memorable morning when she wished to be at school half an hour early, with the exceptional excuse that the King and Queen were coming. Although it was supposedly top secret that the King and Queen were making an inspection of troops in the North Riding, tanks and guns had been ranged along the Castle Howard drive, brushed and polished under the camouflage nets, for days beforehand. Alighting as usual at the Obelisk that day, Katharine found herself in the midst of lines of troops as in a dress rehearsal and, watching from the school ranks at the roadside two hours later, she discovered it was indeed the selfsame spot at which the King and Queen stepped from their car.

"We had a wonderful view," a school historian diligently noted.

"We were in our places early and waited, listening to the military band, until a despatch rider rode up and we heard him say to the officer in charge, 'They are entering the avenue now'. In a few minutes the soldiers lining the road from the Gatehouse took off their caps, and in the distance we heard the sound of cheers. Preceded by two dispatch riders, the royal car slowly drove into sight and many of us saw the King, the Queen and Princess Elizabeth for the first time in our lives." How excited they all were! After inspecting troops and tanks, the royal trio walked past the girls as well as the guns, to speak to the goddesses of the Upper Sixth and enquire which school they were and admire their red cloaks. And for Katharine, all unknowing, it was her first sight of her future in-laws.

As the days lengthened, Katharine argued with juvenile guile that it would patriotically save petrol as well as spare grown-ups time if she could please ride her pony, Greylegs, to school—and, besides, Greylegs needed more exercise. As usual, of course, her pleas were irresistible. And so the landgirls and farming folk used sometimes to see her, riding by way of Wath Wood and Fryton Moor, South Wood and Baxton Howe, five miles through the woods to Castle Howard and five miles back in the late afternoon. She knew every path, every tree. With her fair hair and jaunty red school cloak, she seemed a romantic rider indeed and the Italian prisoners-of-war, working in the fields, would pause to shout admiration at the self-assured little figure, "Ma come è bella! Caro! Caro!", or else greet her with snatches of lyrical song. Tethering Greylegs at the stables, she would change hastily from jodhpurs and then race wildly to tell friends among the boarders her news—how she had seen a "super" tawny owl or glimpsed a fox crossing the track ahead.

Her special friend was a girl named Diana Hynes. They had both entered in the same term, gaining courage from one another at the first Assembly and found their names listed together—D. Hynes, K. Worsley—on the notice-board slip that welcomed the new girls. They sat together in class and played together. On coming to school, Diana had been separated for the first time from her elder sister, Jane, who had gone into the senior Form VB, and Katharine, Kate, (but never Kathie) was a dependable confidante. In the midday break, they chattered wildly on their way to the junior dining-room, between the kitchen and the gym. Both deeply musical, they would have shared piano lessons, if the teacher, Miss Spriggs, had not diplomatically decided that Diana, slightly the elder, was also the more advanced.

Teachers know these intense, spontaneous companionships and how swiftly they sometimes disintegrate into indifference, but the friendship of Kate and Diana remained remarkably constant for two years through the flux of school life. Twelve tennis courts had been marked out on the green lawns of the South Front, and Kate, it seems, was persuasive in booking games with Diana, outside the "Colts" tournament matches. When the girls picked fruit in the walled garden for the school to make jam, the two expertly vied in filling baskets, and it was considered remarkable that the working party sometimes picked a hundred pounds of fruit in an afternoon. Kate shone in cricket, "a terrific slosher", while Diana excelled in lacrosse. Diana wanted to be an artist—and indeed later became a commercial artist—while Kate claimed that she might be a musician. So the friendship prospered, we may judge, with emulation and encouragement on both sides.

The pleasures were seasonal. Katharine asked to be allowed to stay on Saturday afternoons to help potato-picking with the Italian prisoners. Diana, no doubt, persuaded Miss Spriggs to allow Kate to join with boarders when they went to a concert in Malton. At school concerts, they sat side by side to enjoy Mozart and Brahms by the Lydian Trio and the thrilling programme by the Boyd Neel orchestra, one summer afternoon in the Long Gallery. Significant in retrospect, one of their best-enjoyed films at school was *Victoria the Great*. "Historical persons came alive most astonishingly," as a young friend noted at the time.

And then there was the wonder of V.E. Day, Victory in Europe, when after all the eternity of childhood the war at last was over and the facades of Castle Howard were festooned with flags, red cloaks, blue summer tunics, white sheets, everything and anything that could be hung out to give gaiety. The day girl Kate was determined not to miss the fun of the evening dance nor the great bonfire. The Worsleys at Hovingham gathered in quieter celebration while Katharine at school heard the roar of the crowds broadcast from London and shared in the baked potatoes and songs around the beacon fire until the car called to take her home.

The next day, the girls were given lunch packed and told they "might go wherever they liked, on cycle or foot, until the evening". As the school magazine records, "Some cycled to York and saw the decorations. Some went to the Minster, others went to different villages." Kate and the Hyne sisters triumphantly did all three, ending with a superlative late tea at Hovingham.

Everyone wondered what the peace would bring. For Katharine there came suddenly a phase of swift transition, and she spent only three more months at Castle Howard. No more in winter would she whoop on a tray tobogganing down Mausoleum Hill or swim in high summer around the burdened figure of Atlas in the shallow lake of the Fountain. Her cousin, Joy Colegate, had been a boarder at Runton Hill School (when evacuated for a time to the Cotswolds) and all Katharine's insistence to be allowed to join her had been met with, "Perhaps—when the war is over!" And now the war was over at last and Joy, as it happened, had already left Runton—but Kate was in her thirteenth year, her wartime childhood behind her, and no longer to be so readily denied in her constant zest for new experience.

4 What Kate Did Next

Immortal bliss that ne'er will cloy...
Softest repose and blooming joy
In her conspire the soul to charm.
All that can Joy or Love create
Beauteous blessing,
Past expressing
Round the tender Fair one wait

A Song to Mr Handell's Minuett
(The January chimes)

I

Now that she was in her teens, Katharine sometimes sat in for fun at her mother's committee meetings at the long elm table in the Tapestry Hall. "If she would like to watch, please may she?" Lady Worsley would enquire of her guests. With the war ended, it might be useful for Katharine to see the formation of the Welcome Home fund or learn about the plans to stage an opera in the village hall. More often than not, after satisfying her curiosity on what the meeting was all about, she made her excuses and wandered away to more absorbing pleasures.

"We are all too much attached to that table," her father would say, in his joking way, and for a time it was Kate's chore to lay out note-pads and agenda slips on the mellowed polished surface in readiness for the evening's business. Her father would have told her that the great table probably came from the earlier Worsley family home before Hovingham Hall was built and may indeed have dated back to Cromwellian times. On arriving at Runton Hill School, after the long circuitous journey via York and London and Norwich, it was all the more encouraging to discover a very similar table, homely and familiar, to welcome her in the entrance hall. To be sure, it was a table neither so ancient nor so impressive in length and strength but the very style lent a friendly and auspicious touch to her arrival at boarding-school.

Runton Hill was a pleasant turn-of-the-century country house, its entrance forecourt encased in gorse and heather, for its founder and head-mistress at that time would not lift a pruning knife to natural beauty. Katharine was to spend four extremely happy years there, and ultimately, as music secretary, she organized her own committee meetings at its long hall table. Instead of the Imperial tapestries of Hovingham Hall, there was the ageless art-print of the Laughing Cavalier and the Velasquez print of the Infanta Margarita, not unlike Katharine herself. In lieu of Yorkshire rain, there was more often the driving and chilling Norfolk wind from off the North Sea. Yet at Runton Kate discovered that implicit sense of both individuality and kinship that comes of sharing a dormitory with four or five other girls and, in being a boarder and not a day girl, the purposeful contentment of belonging to a small community in her own right. Lady Worsley once noted, with customary precision, that Runton Hill provided "an education varied, humane and individual". From her daughter's viewpoint it was part of her varied education that she experienced the fun of midnight feasts, of biscuits stowed under mattresses and tins of Bournvita concealed in the fire-ladder hatch—and for the first time, too, in that grim post-war period, Katharine discovered the satisfaction of sheer endurance.

As a Senior, an old girl, has written, "Runton in 1945 had little to offer in the way of material comforts; the food was austere and the cold intense. Those in South House on supper duty would hurry along the path in the darkness, while the omnipresent wind snatched the kippers off the trays and whisked them into the surrounding brambles. Heating was practically non-existent owing to the fuel shortage and sometimes we would be compelled to sleep with our bedside mats over our blankets for extra insulation. But somehow we thrived on it; we took pride in being spartan . . ."

The war was over, indeed, but not the intense and continuous hardship that propaganda softly blanketed as "post-war austerity". With clothes rationing at its most stringent, the Sixth Formers pretended it a cult of secret fashion to hold up their much-darned stockings with safety pins and Kate made do for much of her school outfitting with some of her Colegate cousin's "hand-downs . . . of unsuitable size and noticeable age". As an occupant of North House, the older of the school's two houses, she was spared adventures in darkness with wayward kippers. But everyone at Runton Hill was out of doors in all weathers, a fact of life arising less from Miss Harcourt's fresh-air gusto, than from the gradual successful growth of the school within its own grounds, building by building, until it had become a small hamlet.

The story traces back—as with Benenden—to that pioneering girls' school, Wycombe Abbey, which was founded in 1896 to give girls "that discrimination of what is best in the thought and art of other countries as well as their own". Janet Vernon Harcourt had been one of the foundation pupils at Wycombe, eagerly drinking in the sense of adventure that its ideals inculcated, the desire to serve the community and the readiness to live fully, qualities she was one day to strengthen in her own future pupils and not least in today's Duchess of Kent. Subsequently training and working as a teacher, Miss Harcourt decided to instil Wycombe principles in a school of her own and chanced to be staying with a well-to-do uncle and aunt at Runton Old Hall when she heard that a nearby house, the present Runton Hill, was for sale. The key was found hidden under the front-door mat and her aunt was willing to advance the purchase price. A life-sized plaster figure of the dying gladiator, which occupied most of the entrance hall, was moved with difficulty and the school opened five months later with seven pupils.

Within nine years, a new and second house, South House, was built near the old, to be followed in due course by a school hall timbered like a tithe-barn, by separate recreation rooms known to generations of schoolgirls as the Hive and the Bank, by extra class-room buildings and a proliferation or volley of tennis-courts. Moving between North House and the classrooms or down to the cottage called West, the music studio, gave Katharine the familiar, delicious open-air sense of dashing across from Hovingham Hall to the village store. The rivalry between North and South was intense and perennial, especially at mid-term when the entire school, except a minority rescued by being taken out for the day by their parents, repaired to a local ravine known as the Roman Camp to play a desperate game called valley netball. This appears to have been a fiendish St Trinian's rugger of Miss Harcourt's own invention, and one Runton Hill girl, the author Nancy Spain, long recalled it with horror: "I used to spend most of the game face downwards in the bracken, all breath knocked from my body, while the two teams, North *and* South, tramped heavily by on my shoulder blades."

The game was happily long since tempered to a less fearsome contest, and Kate was usually taken out at mid-term by either her mother or one of her aunts and so spared these agonies. But she soon became an aggressive and shining star of lacrosse, revelling in being freed at last from cautious junior school repression. The playing field sloped sharply downhill to the north towards a limitless background of sea and horizon, but Kate could "run like the devil uphill" and emerged in her second year as an heroic captain of the second lacrosse team. Rain and mud could reduce the field to little better than a slippery slope, a handicap to both sides. Kate's early games as team captain were marked by continuous snow, but she had the enterprising idea of playing on the beach at low tide and the cliff slopes made a glorious grandstand for the yelling supporters.

The thickets of rusting iron coastal defences seem to have been cleared faster from north Norfolk than elsewhere and, then as now, the girls usually had the run of empty beaches. Miss Harcourt was opposed to schoolgirl "crocodiles"—the jabbering untidy lines in double file—and, unconventionally, her girls could attend any church they pleased and would often walk into Cromer or Sheringham, taking Sung Eucharist or Low Church very literally in their stride. This freedom also led to the pleasure of cycling to more distant Norfolk churches and thus Katharine, with fair independence, explored a wider radius of countryside. Petrol rationing restricted mid-term expeditions with parents farther afield, but a Worsley family party inspected the Jacobean splendours of Blickling Hall one term and there were memorable school and family picnics to the marshes and dunes at Blakeney Point. If Kate had been taken to Sandringham, she might have caught an early glimpse of the royal home where she would one day be a private Christmas guest; but Sandringham was considered too far, the gardens were never open upon the right days, and we are denied this imaginative footnote to history.

II

"Runton was a place where individuality was fostered and personal eccentricities respected." So one of the Duchess of Kent's school contemporaries has written nostalgically. "Lessons were exciting because we were taught by interesting people, some of our own staff richly eccentric, supplemented by local vicars (who all possessed cars of fabulous antiquity), masters from Gresham's, retired geologists and J.V.H.—Miss Harcourt—herself." It is one of the rewards of the teaching profession that personalities gain a dimension of immortality, and the smallest incidents shine in the lost summers of childhood. A chemistry master, a retired major, came over from Gresham's, the boys' public school at Holt, to give Kate and others highly practical instruction in the making of alcohol and soap. And legends flourished around the figure of Mrs Fisher Prout, the art mistresss, in her "enormous straw hat and long flowing scarlet silk dress" who would lead her students to a meadow at the cliff-top and scatter them with their easels to paint as they wished.

A tidy-minded house mistress had instituted a "confiscations table" where personal things left lying about could be retrieved only under penalties, which included learning passages of poetry on free afternoons or devoting an hour or two at the hated task of weeding in the garden. Essentially tidy and methodical, Kate was rarely involved but in any case she took pride in a garden plot of her own just outside the school hall, where one year she raised a useful mixed crop of flowers and tomatoes.

"I doubt whether she ever had to be punished: she was a very sweet girl", recalls one former Runton Hill teacher. There was nevertheless the historic riot in a form room that occurred when the girls caught sight through the window of a stem of bananas being delivered, *bananas*, the first seen since the war. Those who had never seen a banana rushed forward, the teacher helpless to control the stampede to window and door. And at this juncture the door suddenly opened and in came none other than Miss Harcourt, who quelled the uproar with a glance and characteristically took over the class to teach tropical agriculture for the rest of the period. The lesson was remembered and proved useful in Uganda years later when the Duchess of Kent recollected the unusual knowledge that the banana tree is a herb.

At Queen Margaret's in wartime a solitary banana had been auctioned for charity. At post-war Runton the mystic fruits were soon in sufficient supply to be shared and enjoyed, and other "austerity" hardships were gradually lessened. In Katharine's first term, as we have seen, the fuel shortage was so severe that the girls slept with their bedside mats over their blankets for extra warmth. Things so far improved that during the severe winter of 1947 the girls were permitted to wrap themselves in rugs only during prep and "cocoon-like figures were not allowed at meals". The hardest winter suffered in Britain for sixty-six years served to stress the unexpected geographical truth that there was nothing between Runton Hill and the North Pole but the sea!

Katharine Worsley was noted as exceptionally good in geography, English language and music, and noted, too, as "an exceptionally well-integrated child". Although she personally shone at tennis, she preferred to play rounders for the extra fun, and perhaps as Nancy Spain found, for the confidences exchanged while making "massive daisy chains lying in the hedge". With the junior rounders and junior netball teams, Kate figured in notable games against Holt Hall and she is similarly remembered—"a plump, jolly, vigorous girl"—in the lacrosse matches against Norwich High School and Norwich Ladies.

The surviving school records disclose that she ultimately won her netball and lacrosse colours, but sport, games and lessons alike were obviously still but a fragment of her ever increasing interests. She flourished in the debating club, for instance, in spite of a ban upon all topics of politics and religion! She figured in the "Lit and Dram", and so took part in what one girl calls "an amazing number of plays". Original nativity plays were written and produced for Christmas; there were concert excursions and occasional theatre parties to Norwich in the school bus, and Kate was a knowledgeable organizer of the November 5th school bonfire. "The smell of burning rubber can still vividly recall the tang of scorching goloshes in the tribal dances round the flames," as one girl remembers.

Every schoolgirl in 1947 followed the romance of Princess Elizabeth and Prince Philip, and Katharine watched the school film of the royal wedding unaware how closely the ceremonial and pageantry would be followed in her own. The long-awaited occasion of the annual school dance brought a traditional contingent of polite young partners from Gresham's. "It is a truth universally acknowledged," wrote a young authoress in the *Runton Hill Gazette* "that every Gresham's boy on attaining the VIth form must be in want of a girl ... The junior ladies of Runton found their nerves in a great flutter, but ... the excitement of so many handsome jerseys and the extreme courtesy of their wearers made the young ladies quite equal to the occasion."

Scrooge was read just before the break-up for Christmas, and the carol service with the school orchestra must have been another exciting and significant annual event of Katharine's school year. Runton Hill was always particularly strong in music, as it is today, with teachers coming in for the pianoforte, violin and viola, clarinet, oboe, bassoon, and flute and—a more modern note—the guitar. In her last autumn term, Kate was formally elected music secretary, and her organized programme visits to recitals in Norwich and choral and orchestral concerts at Gresham's were to stand her in good stead as training for the series of Hovingham festivals to follow.

Staged for Parents' Day, the summer play at Runton Hill made use of a remarkable natural feature, a deep-hollowed dell where seats had been scooped out bank by bank to form an ampitheatre and in this natural setting, year by year, the repertoire ranged from Shakespeare to Benjamin Britten. Striding the idyllic stage, Kate at sixteen played Sebastian in *Twelfth Night*, a slimmer Kate than of old, looking well in boyish costume. The part, not too exacting, had been cast with precision by the elocution mistress and producer, well aware that if rehearsals clashed with Katharine's musical interests, music might take priority. The cry "Where's Kate?" was invariably answered with "Down at West!" where, sure enough, the sound of Mozart proclaimed that "K. Worsley" was hogging a practice room.

As at Hovingham, the ancient village church lay scarcely a hundred yards away and similarly reached through a short cut by the tennis courts, just as at home, and here, shortly after her sixteenth birthday, Katharine was confirmed by the Bishop of Norwich. During the holidays, her elders noticed her widening horizons. There were local boys whose fortunes she had followed with interest, watching their prowess at the Malton grammar school sports, but she had obviously grown out of, and almost forgotten, this or that fascination. She had been "a keen member of the Pony Club", as her mother said, but local gymkhanas saw little of her now and the dust gathered on her share of rosettes. But meanwhile she loved riding over the old familiar tracks, she eagerly cajoled her brothers into tennis matches—and a new world of acquaintances opened in all the friends they brought home from Oxford.

Rather abruptly, in the autumn term of 1949, Katharine realized that her schooldays—once so eternal—were "closing in". She would never be head girl or even head of her house. The blue circle on her grey-blue tunic as captain of the first lacrosse XII would have to suffice. Asked what she might like to do on leaving school, the pleasure she took in her young cousins, Auntie Joyce's children, two-year-old Tommy and seven-year-old Susan, came foremost to mind, and she vaguely suggested "something to do with looking after children".

Sitting for her Oxford and Cambridge general schools certificate, Katharine gained a pass in oral French and a "very good" for English literature. "Far better than average", Miss Harcourt perhaps commended her, turning from her oak desk at a farewell interview. The head's study then seemed "so dark and cramped, still with its bare oak floors and awful Turkey carpets", as the present head mistress has grimly noted, and change was near. Katharine's school-leaving indeed coincided with Miss Harcourt's own retirement.

Lady Worsley was guest speaker at that last speech day and gracefully expressed the appreciation of parents of "the high standard attained by the school in many spheres". At the ensuing concert Katharine played a movement of a Mozart concerto, as if to conclude her schooldays with a flourish of applause. And then the farewells were said, the Cromer taxi was waiting—and so no longer "the background music of the sea and the nearer music of the pines", the sudden squalls shaking the dormitory windows, the enduring wind to blow away cobwebs and confidences alike as one walked below the cliffs along the beach . . .

III

Katharine had often promised her brothers, "I'll get to Oxford before you do!" It was a family joke, of course, based on the years that a young man had to give to his country in those days of "national service", and when the boys all duly matriculated, the promise became a wry sisterly threat, "Wait until I come up!" When Katharine left Runton Hill, her eldest brother, Marcus, eight years her senior, had already served in the Green Howards, from which he was romantically seconded to the Royal West African Frontier Force, and he had returned to take an honours degree in modern history at New College. Over Christmas, he broke the news that he hoped to join the B.B.C. as a programme assistant early in the New Year, probably in the European Service. And this left Oliver and John still at Trinity as the decisive, all-compelling factor in Kate's eager wish to get to Oxford before they, too, came down.

Miss Harcourt had many Oxford connections and may well have recommended Miss A. E. Hubler's finishing school at 22 Merton Street. Just off "The High", Mme. Hubler's establishment had an impeccable reputation, both among the undergrads for its known populace of pretty girls and among parents—including some North Riding neighbours—who were impressed by the poise and good sense which their daughters undoubtedly acquired during a few semi-adult months in Oxford.

Seeking out Merton Street today, one finds one of those change-
less cobbled byways that visitors love to photograph, winding
between the creamy facades of Oriel and the stout flint walls of the
grounds of Merton College. To the left there comes a tender cluster
of Georgian cottages with their steps and rails and delicate sash-
windows, and then the lane winds to the north and Number 22
proves to be one of a terrace of tall and narrow four-storey
buildings in the gabled and ornate Dutch style that Norman Shaw
popularized at the turn of the century.

Paying a preliminary visit, Lady Worsley found the house curiously familiar, reminding her pleasantly of her own girlhood days.
It belonged indeed to the same genre as her childhood home in
Wetherby Gardens and the interior, though smaller, resembled her
parents' later house in Harrington Gardens. Even the staircase was
friendly and akin in design, to the white-painted bannisters and
polished mahogany rail, like the familiar stairs she had climbed so
often before. We are all susceptible to such gentle suggestions and,
perhaps remembering a quality of loneliness in her own childhood,
Lady Worsley felt grateful that her daughter would again have the
opportunity to make many more friends.

And so for the first time in her life, Katharine went to live in a
house in the middle of a town, in a markedly feminine household,
with disciplines as regulated as its chiming clock and with friendships varied as the footsteps up and down the stairs. From its front
windows, Number 22 gazed across Merton Street to the elaborate
wrought-iron entrance gates and green forecourt of the Examination
Schools. At the back, to the east, beyond a pocket lawn, the leaded
bedroom windows surveyed the gardens of Merton and the soaring
tower of Magdalen. On May Day this led to a flurry among Miss
Hubler's pupils, for this is the morning when a choir traditionally
salutes the sunrise by singing a seventeenth-century hymn from the
top of Magdalen Tower, and it would have been disgraceful to miss
the spectacle by lying abed.

At about 4.30 a.m. a confusion of young ladies in dressing-gowns
invaded the upper bedrooms to crowd at the windows to see what
they could. In harsh reality the early risers' award was little more
than a too distant view of the medieval caps of the choir crowded

like buttons between the Magdalen pinnacles, and a tiny baton waving frantically at the singers' heads. Equally little was to be heard at that distance unless the young ladies could refrain from yawns and witticisms and bring themselves to keep quiet. But it was the occasion that mattered, and while some returned sleepily to their pillows, the braver souls, Kate among them that year, dressed and went out for an early morning walk in the Meadows, fresh in the dew. Memories are made of such moments.

The school was "select", so much so that there were in fact only eight pupils. In Kate's day, in Miss Hubler's recollection, these included Tina Goschen, Elizabeth James, Elizabeth Messel—a distant cousin of Lord Snowdon—with one of Lord Londonderry's daughters and the daughter of Viscount Mountgarret. "I had no staff for teaching", Miss Hubler notes. "The girls attended some lectures and studied French literature, French history, French painting and architecture with me." Her curriculum however also included current affairs and household management, with some of the skills she considered essential in business life. On the first floor, a splendid room with a notable bay window would serve for an hour as a salon for a talk on Georgian furniture and then as a classroom for a demonstration of dressmaking and practical couture. The French lady-cook, Marcelle Powell, evidently played some part in lessons on cookery. Prim visits were conducted to the Ashmolean Museum, an occasion when some girls played absentee and would lose themselves in the Cornmarket shopping crowds. But most afternoons were free from the treadmill of tuition.

Katharine continued her music studies with advanced lessons with a Viennese lady two or three times a week, having promised her father that she meant to work. And yet Oxford was hers, in all its infinite variety, the college quadrangles, the exquisite chapels; and hers especially the atmosphere of youth, of living freely with her contemporaries in their exclusive and almost unfettered world. The undergrads of 1950 were a more mature and orderly generation than today, more sophisticated, perhaps, after the conscript realities of military service. Oliver Worsley, for example, had seen service with the King's Royal Rifles before matriculating at Trinity in the autumn of 1948. Now he was reading agriculture, and Kate knew precisely where she would find him, in the long pale galleries of the Bodleian, and knew almost the minute when he would close his books with a sigh of satisfaction, his stint accomplished.

She found it amusing, too, to find John at his own remote library desk, reading history. Though both were at Trinity, the two brothers kept their distance when needful, wary of disturbing one another's studies. But Oxford is a place for learning and a place for play. In February, Katharine celebrated her seventeenth birthday— and, of course, Oliver's twenty-third—with a wonderful party at the latter's digs. John merrily asserted that he had only been waiting around in Oxford for this. He had in fact gained his honours degree the previous term and he went down in March, having completed nine terms of residence. Even more than Katharine, he enjoyed an astonishing facility of making friends everywhere, and life was quieter without him.

Kate, Oliver and John, the three Worsleys, had been one of the few family trios at Oxford—but now they were two. Food ration-ing still persisted and Oliver usually ate in hall, where the food was rated "not bad"; Miss Hubler, too, kept a good table, all things considered. Yet sometimes, for the sheer fun of knowing everything that went on, Kate and Oliver joined, "the queue of undergraduates winding submissively in the gloom round the steps of the Town Hall" to receive the British Restaurant two-course lunch for 1s 3d. They occasionally "went Dutch" to theatres and concerts together, each paying their share. Strangers were apt to envy Oliver the company of the pretty blonde, unaware she was his sister. As John had done, he hovered protectively at times, aware that amid his contingent of ex-Army friends she was one of the youngest and prettiest girls in sight.

Katharine none the less flung off her guardian and enjoyed herself uninhibitedly during the parties and dances of Commemoration week. There was no shortage of not-too-serious partners for the College balls nor lack of companions for the long afternoons of punting on the Char. She could vicariously experience the solem-nity of graduation, watching Oliver receive his Honours degree later on in the time-hallowed setting of the Sheldonian. And then

Oliver, too, went down, full of plans for the farming responsibilities he was to take over gradually from his father, and one learns that Kate "whisked about enjoyably" during the long vacation, plied with inexhaustible house-party invitations but staying at home for the Hovingham Hall garden fete, where she ran a games stall and had successfully cajoled her parents into hiring Kay's Orchestra for dancing on the lawns.

Although it had appeared that this might signal the conclusion of her Oxford adventure, she nevertheless returned there contentedly for the Michaelmas term. There were already new faces at Miss Hubler's, new friends to initiate into the richer interests of Oxford life, and Kate felt mature and experienced as she seriously attempted at last to make up her mind about her future career.

IV

"Please don't let your daughter stay at home," Miss Brown, the head-mistress at Queen Margaret's, had said long ago at a parents' day at Castle Howard. "You want to give them pleasure and freedom—and it is so easy for them to drift into doing nothing very particular. The world of hard work and strenuous endeavour alike hold the secret of happiness, and that service is alone perfect freedom." The words had struck a responsive chord with Lady Worsley and the echoes still lingered. She could not but feel tremors of anxiety lest her daughter should "moon about" at Hovingham, her academic education vaguely concluded, while the question of any future career remained unresolved. Yet Katharine was never one to mark time. She was more apt to whirl from one engrossing interest to another, energetic and decisive, and often impulsive.

According to Miss Hubler, there was some question of Kate spending a year at Benenden as if to take an entrance exam for one of the Oxford women's colleges. Oxford was evidently still in mind. But if there were any parental discussions, their subject returned home for Christmas in no mood for any more schooling. Would it not be absurd to be a new girl again when practically eighteen? And besides, after Runton Hill and Oxford, had she not already been away from home for far too long?

As it happened, her beloved Aunt Joyce had just had another baby, a sister to join young Tommy and Susan. "An angel!" said Kate, fervently, on first taking this new Worsley in her arms, and so the infant was named Angela, and the young name-giver also appointed herself an honorary nursery assistant. It was alleged light-heartedly that whenever Katharine rode over to Aunt Joyce at Cawton Hall she assuredly had a nursing apron, baby powder and safety-pins in a saddle-bag. As Mrs Worsley has said, the sponsorship of her children has followed a pattern, the three Worsley brothers being godparents to her three older children, "so that each has an older cousin as a godparent". Thus Susan is Marcus's god-daughter, Thomas is Oliver's godson and Angela is John's god-daughter. And in due course, in Coronation year, Katharine was to become godmother to the youngest girl, Diana Rosalind.

Yet Angela was only three weeks old when Sir William Worsley perceived that Katharine had other things on her mind. The New Year of 1951 was ushered in with particular eclat, for it was to witness the nation-wide celebrations of the Festival of Britain. The centenary of the 1851 exhibition was to be linked with national commemoration of the supposed milestone of postwar recovery and countless locally sponsored events were to illustrate the theme, "both our pride in our past and our faith in the future" as Sir Gerald Barry put it. Hovingham had scarcely begun to envisage its local plans, and Kate and Oliver broached the subject one evening. Why not revive the Hovingham Festival itself?

Over forty years had elapsed since the last of those wonderful gatherings in the Riding School and Sir William pretended jokingly that he was the only member of the family who remembered it. But Kate in fact could "see it all", as clearly as her father or her elder Aunt Winifred. She had been poring over the old programmes and photographs, browsing through Lady Macdonald's reminiscences and talking to the elderly folk who remembered, as one said, how the festivals had spread an annual electric web of excitement through the North Riding.

A plaque commemorating the events had been placed in the entrance arch of the Riding School but it was no use, Kate pointed out, having a tablet to "all who made music here" if one could never make music again. Her enthusiasm, as ever, was eloquent and persuasive and it needed only her parents' approval to set the wheels in motion. John had already drawn up estimates of cost and the receipts that would accrue to charity. Oliver had successfully sounded public opinion. Katharine intended "the mixture as before, of London professionals and the best local talent" and by mid-February she had approached the London concert agents with such undiluted verve and energy that plans were sufficiently firm for the revival of the Festival to be made public.

Impresarios of the calibre of Harold Holt and Harold Fielding never knew that they were conducting a correspondence on fees and availabilities with a girl of only just on eighteen. An appointed Festival committee met at the refectory table in the Tapestry Hall, but Kate was the effective acting secretary, translating plans into correspondence and agreements, and her father had only to add his signature to the letters after she had drafted and redrafted them on the big typewriter in his study.

This was also the year of Kate's coming-out, her social début when her parents rented a London house for a month to give the dances and parties then considered inseparable from launching a daughter into the social pleasures of London. But Kate, though she enjoyed herself, was not particularly interested. She was for ever on the telephone to Oliver at Hovingham. Her parents were secretly amused at her command of concert jargon as she talked of bookings and engagements, cancellations and deputies, or the travel arrangements for a marionette troupe and an unexpected shortage of grand pianos. She was radiant one morning on being able to announce that the Viennese organist, Susi Jeans, had consented to give an organ recital in Hovingham church, and that the Griller Quartet had been "triumphantly secured" for a programme of Beethoven and Schubert in the Riding School.

Aiming high, Kate had talked of choirs and orchestras which might give works by local composers. Lady Worsley, apparently, proposed that the children of the village school might make an effective contribution and, deciding that they should sing Mozart, suitably "produced" and costumed, her daughter worked exuberantly as a rehearsal assistant and accompanist, training the young country children to sing the Noble Lady chorus from *The Marriage of Figaro*. A raid upon the attics of Hovingham Hall in search of a collection of music stands led to the wonderful discovery of an old harpsichord, swaddled beneath cobwebs and sacking. The mellow woods of the case could still glow to a polishing finger-tip, the keys still respond and a Scarborough expert confirmed that the instrument could be successfully reconditioned, and Katharine declared that it would have been worth all the work of the Festival for that find alone.

In June, 1951, Sir William Worsley was appointed Lord Lieutenant of the North Riding, following the retirement of the Marquis of Zetland. He had learned of the King's nomination some months earlier, and bore the distinction with modest pride. His family, too, were all deeply conscious of the dignity conferred upon him, but the announcement only a month before the Festival led inevitably to a barrage of outrageous youthful jokes which he endured with good humour. The Lord Lieutenant is officially responsible for the maintenance of public order and was empowered to raise the militia if the Festival caused a riot, so Kate had better beware! He also had powers to appoint magistrates for the county bench, the boys hilariously pointed out, who would no doubt inflict fearful sentences for mismanagement or wasted time. As it turned out, on the Festival opening night, the Sovereign's newly appointed representative was laid up in bed with a chill, and it was Marcus who presided over the hospitality for the visiting artistes and Oliver who acted as compère, while Kate excitedly watched the Riding School filling to capacity. Everything was a huge success, not least a puppet opera wonderfully contrived by the Lanchester Marionettes and New English Singers. "Next time," Lady Worsley complimented her flushed and elated daughter, "We shall have singers from Glyndebourne, you'll see!"—and so it proved.

V

At the edge of the old City of York, running southwest from Micklegate Bar, there is a street optimistically named Blossom Street, lined by small shops and repair garages, broad and busy. Turning slightly uphill, the thoroughfare more truthfully changes its name to The Mount, and at this point there stands a long, low white house, withdrawn a little from the roar and rush of the traffic, sheltered behind shrubs of privet and laurel. The building is possibly of Georgian date, faced with Regency stucco, but the doors and windows have been garnished with recent enthusiasm in pale blue and yellow paintwork. A casual passer-by might notice no more than the name, "St Stephen's" or the coin slot in the wall with the hopeful words "Thank You". A signboard announces the hours of a Spastics Club and indicates the door of a brick-built wing round the corner. But you have to see the children playing on the garden lawn at the back to know that this is St Stephen's Children's Home, and only long-established local folk remember that this is where today's Duchess of Kent once tended hearths and swept floors, enacting a variant of her own on the theme of Cinderella.

The local authority lists St Stephen's as "an independent voluntary children's home, for boys and girls aged from 3 upwards", but it began as an orphanage and home for waifs and foundlings in the days when Katharine's grandfather, Sir William Henry Worsley, sent a foundation cheque as a thank-offering for the birth of his first-born child, and it has been a favourite charity of the Worsley family ever since. A Worsley wing was added for another family commemoration, and a Brotherton wing built on when Katharine's uncle, Charles Brotherton, rejoiced in turn in a child of his own. St Stephen's is one of the many small unnoticed institutions of quiet good-doing, its special province being "bereft children, illegits, children in need of care", as one young helper explains, perhaps fostering a young family while the mother is in maternity hospital or else looking after a small child whose mother necessarily works away from home.

As long as she could remember, Katharine had turned out her nursery cupboard twice a year, looking for surplus—and often not-so-surplus— toys for St Stephen's. Later on, she made up Christmas parcels for the home and expertly packed "boxes" for the St Stephen's bazaars. Her mother was chairman of the little managing committee and, one evening in 1951, Lady Worsley returned home more concerned than usual with the problem of staff holidays. The difficulty was that the children were usually given an annual seaside holiday at an old house in Filey. One or two of the St Stephen's staff had to remain in York, there was the added complication of personal staff holidays, and the fine mesh of arrangements was jeopardized by the need of coping with electricians who were preparing to wire the Filey house, Katharine joined in the conversation on these perplexities and suddenly volunteered, "But it's simple. Couldn't I help out?"

The extra pair of hands made all the difference. While Kate and another helper took their twenty little girls down to the beach, the housekeeper coped with meals and bed-making and the inevitable clearing up behind the workmen. When the holidays ended, Kate went to St Stephen's, having attached herself as if the "helping out" might go on for years. She helped, indeed, with everything, bathing and dressing the younger children, helping with the breakfast and the shopping, the classes and games, the nursing and mending. Mrs Elsie Cobb, the matron, remembers her as "always happy, singing about the place, almost a child herself. There was nothing she wouldn't do. She adored the children, and they idolised her."

A member of the family was under the impression that Kate "shared a flat" in Blossom Street. This was perhaps the chill upper staff flat which she shared for a time, living in. The cook of those days, Mrs Hart, recalls her helping in the kitchen, at the stove and washing-up sink, and the muddle they were all in, literally walking the plank, while workmen were renewing the kitchen floor. "I've learned to cook at school and at home," said Katharine. "Now I'm learning catering under difficulties." If a child were physically sick, Kate took it for granted that, being on hand, she should clear up the mess. An elder woman on the staff demurred that one unpleasant job "wasn't expected" of a young volunteer. "Someone's got to do it," said Kate cheerfully, vigorously wielding her scrubbing brush.

There were always such tasks, sinks to be cleaned, socks to be mended, tiny shoes to be taken to the cobbler. The children apart, the old house itself needed tending, with walls to be washed clean of finger-marks, and troublesome nails to be hammered back. Katharine's aunt, Victoria King-Farlow, may have had St Stephen's in mind when she wrote of the "odd bits of moulding in unexpected places", the "unsuitable pieces of period furniture in odd corners". A chair-leg was loose and Kate mysteriously "just happened to have the glue" to mend it. A Christmas donation arrived from the Young Conservatives, subtly directed and explained by the fact that Kate had spent her "evening off" with their carol-singers.

The Northern Command that year "happened" to send a Christmas tree laden with gifts, and Kate explained at home that she would be on duty on Christmas Day. There were indeed forty at the St Stephen's party, the "delight of the children unbounded", not to mention the unfeigned happiness of more than a dozen "old girls" who had neither homes nor close relatives of their own. Characteristically, Kate was remembered "happy and thoughtful in turn", when Oliver called for her by car later in the day to take her to the family party at Hovingham Hall.

The St Stephen annual report mentions that, during Kate's year, the Filey house was "made much more cheerful and homelike" and there is mention of the "treats of various kinds" with which helpers created the happiness of the bereft children. Lady Worsley recollects her daughter often bringing "some of the children home for weekends", weekends that one Stephen's child recalled years later as "sunny holidays in a childhood paradise".

Kate was working at the home in February, 1952, when the radio programmes were suddenly interrupted and the solemn news came of the death of King George VI at Sandringham. To three or four of the older girls who questioned her she tried to explain what the death of a king might mean and what duties would fall around the young Queen who was hurrying home even then from East Africa. Katharine was nineteen that month, celebrating with a birthday tea at St Stephen's, and a birthday party at her own home in the evening. An anniversary dance that had been planned at the Hall seemed inappropriate at the home of the Lord Lieutenant at a time of national mourning and under the circumstances it was postponed until June.

Like all young people, Kate felt caught up in the events of Accession Year. The new Queen was only in her mid-twenties; the newspapers were talking already of a new Elizabethan age, and from month to month the press recorded royal events with exceptional coverage. In October, Kate thus read with interest that the young Duke of Kent was accompanying his mother on her official tour of Malaya and the

Far East. "The Boy Duke grows up", proclaimed a headline that may
have caught her eye. And then in March, 1953, just after her twentieth
birthday, every newspaper in the land carried a photograph of the
young Duke walking behind the gun-carriage at the funeral of Queen
Mary. At his side walked the Duke of Edinburgh, the Duke of
Windsor and the Duke of Gloucester, all in Service uniform. The
Duke of Kent wore morning dress, a youthful schoolboy figure, slim
and vulnerable and yet somehow courageous in that long ordeal of
public homage. It was a photograph that Katharine long remembered
with compassion, a quality not unimportant, perhaps, in the inner ties
of affection and respect.

5 London and Yorkshire

My Goddess Celia, Heavenly Fair,
As lilies Sweet, as soft as Air;
Let loose thy tresses, Spread thy charms,
And to my love give fresh alarms.

Celia the Fair
(The November chimes)

I

Prince Edward of Kent, the present Duke, was born on October 9th, 1935, at Number 3 Belgrave Square. He uttered his first robust cry at two o'clock in the morning in the elegant canopied Directoire bed where his sister was to be born on Christmas Day the following year and, in accordance with the tradition then still observed, the Home Secretary, Sir John Simon, was present in the house at the time, having wearily travelled up after midnight from his home in Surrey. Even at that hour a small crowd waited for news outside in the square, so great was the popularity of the young parents, the Duke and Duchess of Kent, and so deep the public interest in the arrival of their first child. Born seventh in succession to the Throne, the new baby was the first grandson in the male line of King George V and Queen Mary, who were also his principal sponsors when he was baptized in the private chapel at Buckingham Palace and endowed with the resounding royal names of Edward George Nicholas Paul Patrick.

By coincidence, Prince Edward was born in the self-same house in which his great-great-great-grandmother, another Duchess of Kent, mother of Queen Victoria, had been living nearly a century earlier, but this was indeed the merest chance. The modern Kents had in fact leased the house furnished from Lady Juliet Duff not many months before, and the two royal lines of Kent had nothing but their remote kinship in common. The royal ducal title itself, originating in the days of William the Conqueror, had been briefly renewed in the reign of

Queen Anne and again for the fourth son of George III, the Duke of Kent and Strathearn and Earl of Dublin, whose chief claim to fame was that his daughter, Victoria, became heiress to the Crown. Then the dukedom was auspiciously revived in 1934 when King George V accorded his own fourth son, Prince George, the new creation of "Duke of Kent, Earl of St Andrews and Baron Downpatrick".

Nine days later, on November 29th, 1934, the new Duke married the lovely Princess Marina of Greece and Denmark and so left Westminster Abbey with a new royal Duchess whose beauty, modesty and charm had quickly established her in public affection. Prince George was often considered the most good-looking, personable and gifted of all the four royal brothers, King George V's sons, "sharply different in outlook and temperament from the rest of us", as the Duke of Windsor has said, "possessed of unusual charm of manner and a quick sense of humour, talented in many directions". When this fun-loving, forward-looking and popular prince fell ardently in love with an extremely pretty but also extremely shy princess, and when it leaked out that he had romantically proposed at a family shooting lodge in the mountains of Yugoslavia, general delight had known no bounds.

Though unfamiliar to the public, Princess Marina had often visited England, but when she came to London after her betrothal, flowers were flung in front of her car by the enthusiastic crowds. An unusual tribute even in the bright pre-war era of royalty, this was one of the last occasions when flowers were tossed in front of royal cars in London, and the wedding in Westminster Abbey was the first such occasion of pageantry for more than ten years and was the first to be broadcast by sound radio. "Never in history has a marriage been attended by so vast a company," said the Archbishop of Canterbury, the same Archbishop Lang who had officiated at Lady Worsley's wedding. "The whole nation are the wedding guests." The young couple were also married by Greek Orthodox rites in the private chapel of Buckingham Palace, and when bride and groom appeared on the Palace balcony, the cheering, waving crowds were the largest and happiest throng London had seen for many a long day. Ten months after the wedding, Prince Edward of Kent was born as the heir to this tremendous display of public affection.

He was still not two months old when his nanny, Ethel Smith, had to develop subtle techniques to ward off photographers, swaddling and over-wrapping him in shawls when wheeling him out in his pram for an airing under the plane-trees of Belgrave Square or a street or two beyond into Hyde Park. The height of the boundary walls and fencing at Coppins, the Kents' country home in Buckinghamshire, had to be strategically increased. Yet no one took more photographs with more pride than the young Duke of Kent himself, who endearingly always had snapshots of the baby to show his friends and built up a huge family collection. His camera was particularly busy in June, 1939, with snaps to show family relatives at the wedding festivities of Princess Irene of Greece. Lacking the gift of prevision, it was left only to his mind's eye to retain the scoop of the year, for this was just after his tour of Yorkshire and, as we remember, he had all unknowingly met his son's future wife, little six-year-old Katharine Worsley, when visiting Hovingham only two days earlier.

Then the war eclipsed the Kent children, Prince Edward and Princess Alexandra alike, and they disappeared from the rationed and shrinking pages of the newspapers. They were taken to shelter in the Sandringham cellars when the first air-raid sirens wailed on the day war broke out, and they accompanied Queen Mary the following day into her wartime retreat at Badminton House. Both the youngsters revelled in the ever-changing joys of country life, "searching for truant hens' eggs, gathering windfall apples, helping to pick berries, romping in the straw in the great barns", as I once wrote, the precise background that Katharine Worsley herself enjoyed at Hovingham. They returned to Coppins for a time shortly after their brother, Prince Michael of Kent, was born on July 4th, 1942, and seven weeks later they were at Wilton sharing a summer holiday with the Herbert children, when they had to be told the terrible truth that they would never see their father again.

In the midst of all the tragedies of the war, the public were stunned at the news that the handsome and popular Duke of Kent had been killed. He was in only his fortieth year. He had been flying to Iceland while on active service with the R.A.F., and his plane had crashed on a remote moor in north-west Scotland with only one survivor. The children "could not yet realize the meaning of the loss they had sustained", wrote Lady Cynthia Colville, whose harrowing task it had been to break the tragic news to Queen Mary. But the six-year-old Prince Edward was now Duke of Kent, living henceforth in his dead father's shadow, his boyhood never more to be entirely free of the awareness of the deep grief of his mother's bereavement.

At the age of nine he went to Ludgrove preparatory school, near Wokingham. His name had been put down for Eton at his birth and also accordingly put down for Ludgrove as an indispensable preliminary. This strikes a remindful chord, for the Worsley brothers were also Ludgrove boys, though belonging to a schoolboy "generation" of at least five years earlier. Their names shone on commemorative plaques of bygone cricket teams or were to be seen in back files of the school magazine, if the young Duke ever had time to browse through them. His sister occupied his attention with a daily letter from home, until adults questioned the prudence of the ceaseless correspondence and the impetuous stream was reduced. When the Duke of Kent entered Eton in 1948, it was again in the wake of the Worsleys, although by then all three brothers had shaken the green blades of the playing fields off their feet, to go on in their various ways to Oxford or to Army service.

Young "Eddie Kent" was, in fact, not as happy as the Worsleys at Eton. He suffered from allergic asthma and sinus trouble, and within two years it was thought better for him to go to the more healthy air of Le Rosey, the boys' school on Lake Geneva, where he made innumerable friends, among them the Prince Karim Aga Khan and others with whom the Duke has never lost touch. It might require a learned treatise, preferably by an American sociologist, to trace the web of social connections spun from the schoolboy friendships struck up in the common-rooms of Ludgrove and the houses of Eton and Le Rosey. Yet one finds the fine-spun links constantly bridging the gulfs of acquaintance.

It happened in 1952, for instance, that Miss Iris Peake, daughter of Mr Osbert Peake, then Minister of Social Insurance, was appointed lady in waiting to Princess Margaret. The Peakes lived near Northallerton and were on long-standing neighbourly terms with the Worsleys. Iris's brother, Martin, had been at Eton and Trinity with Oliver, who in due turn met his future wife through the Peakes and—some years after Katharine's own marriage—Martin's little daughter, Henrietta, was a bridal attendant at Oliver's wedding. Katharine in turn was enmeshed in these friendships. We may go further and discover that Oliver's agricultural partner, Joe Goodhart, ultimately married Fiona Bowes-Lyon, a relative of the Queen, a match that might not have come about but for the links through Katharine. Yet this is glancing too far ahead and in 1952 there were more immediate and perceptible tremors of events to come. Among the weekly papers delivered to Hovingham Hall, Katharine particularly watched *Picture Post*, in case they ever devoted an article to Hovingham, as they had done once before, and in Coronation year she would have noticed a three-page feature that marked the conclusion of the Duke of Kent's schooldays at Le Rosey. She did not clip the pages and indeed quite forgot them, only to be delighted years later to discover that Princess Marina's secretary, Sir Philip Hay, still had them on file.

Sir William and Lady Worsley were Coronation guests in Westminster Abbey by virtue of the Lord-Lieutenancy, taking their distant seats well before 8 a.m., and thankful for once for the Yorkshire habit of early rising. The strains of the hidden orchestra, the arrival of foreign dignitaries, the assembly of the Dean and Prebendaries, the constant observation of robes and incidents passed the long waiting time. They watched the procession of members of the Royal Family, romantic and costumed figures advancing along an aisle of blue and gold, the Duke of Kent's grouping in itself perfect and memorable, the youthful Duke in his robes, his coronet carried by a page. Much later in the ceremony, the Duke of Kent had his own role to play, following the Duke of Edinburgh and the Duke of Gloucester as the third royal duke to do homage to the crowned Queen, kneeling as she sat upon the Throne. From where they sat, the Worsleys could not notice his one trivial slip, that of forgetting he still wore his glove as he took the hand of the Queen. Nor could they know that within eight years to the week, in their own York Minster, they would tenderly watch the young Duke taking their daughter's hand in marriage.

II

Katharine revelled in the events of London in that year of Coronation. She watched the wonderful ceremony itself on television with a group of friends at John's flat in Curzon Street and then they rushed to Hyde Park to watch the Queen in the Gold State Coach riding by in the rain. That evening, they joined the happy crowds that passed and repassed under those slender and lovely opalescent arches in the Mall. Somewhere in the throng the Duke of Kent and his sister were there as well, with groups of friends, and it is pleasant to reflect that on that night of rejoicing, the Duke of Kent and his Katharine may have unknowingly encountered one another amid the smiles and laughter of the passing thousands. It was during this day of fun and excitement, if not a little earlier, that Kate first met Carolyn Hardinge, whom John married in Montreal the following year. Everything seemed in flux in that Coronation atmosphere. Even Marcus, more studious and settled than his younger brothers, talked of leaving the B.B.C. and trying for Parliament. Each day appeared to glow with the prospect of new friends, fresh viewpoints and new beginnings. Or was this urgent sense of novelty and change, for Kate, merely the first fruits of being twenty and being in London?

"A vivacious girl, sparkling with her love of music and the theatre and her interest in people", a friend notes some first impressions of this time. "One felt qualities of deep reserve behind the effervescence, her plans not mere wistfulness but based on a fund of considerable commonsense." Meeting so many of her friends and acquaintances in London, Kate said lightly that she wanted to stay there for ever, although in reality she was bent on fulfilling a plan for a full year of grown-up enjoyable independence in town, a full year and no more.

Her year at St Stephen's ended by the same easy mutual agreement with which it began, and her thoughts turned to fuller, more expert work with children. Just as John and Oliver had acted as her Oxford mentors, so Marcus and John now kept a brotherly eye on her, Marcus from his flat in Montague Street, not too far from the B.B.C., and John in Mayfair. Once Kate had made up her mind what she wanted to do, it was all smooth sailing. In particular, Marcus had "some conversation" with the Eden family, whom they all knew well. Patricia, Lady Eden—sister-in-law of Sir Anthony Eden and mother of the present ninth baronet—had gained remarkable success with a private day school for girls which she had founded some five years earlier at the heart of one of the most exclusive residential districts of Kensington. The school took girls from the ages of four to twelve, with just a few boys aged four to five. It was a difficulty, according to Lady Eden, that Miss Worsley was completely untrained, but a kindergarten helper was to leave at the summer holidays and it was agreed Katharine should take her place in the autumn at a nominal salary of £12 per month.

Of all her Kensington memories, Kate was never to forget her preliminary visit to Lady Eden's, walking along Victoria Road, with all the gardens bright with summer flowers, to the big fresh-painted house halfway down on the corner. A secluded street of fanciful stucco Regency villas, confected with bow-fronts and balconies, diminutive domes and vine-hung porticoes, Victoria Road is still endearingly rural. Not half a mile from Kensington Palace, it seems appropriate that the small girls at Lady Eden's are taught to drop curtseys in greeting, and one visitor has written of her impressions of "boaters, bulb jars, tadpoles, unchipped paint, *Men of Harlech* sung in unison", but above all of "bobbing girls in blue" as the children curtseyed on introduction.

"My aim is a happy atmosphere. Happy children learn more quickly", Lady Eden would say to fond mothers. "Manners and deportment are of great importance here. Cleanliness, like tidiness, is a part of education . . ." No doubt these remarks were echoed to Miss Worsley. Her lack of a Montessori diploma or a Froebel certificate could be equated against her undeniable social standing. The trim school uniform at Lady Eden's—white-trimmed blue frocks, the white socks, white gloves, ribboned boater—was not less distinctive than the "twin set and pearls" of the teaching staff. "I don't *blame*," said Lady Eden, with one of her smiles, on Katharine's first day, "We give praise whenever possible. Anyway, a little child is usually so upset if it has offended you."

Katharine understood this well, and Lady Eden had been impressed by her practical experience at St Stephen's in handling the youngest

children. The summer was notable for a holiday with Kate's Colegate
cousins in the Isle of Wight, the last summer when all the Colegates
would be together as a family group, and then she almost jubilantly
started work for the autumn term. For local parents, it was an asset of
the school that classes were small, with a teacher on average to every
ten pupils, and a staff of seventeen or so to the 160 children in
Katharine's time. The school was noted, moreover, for its excellence
in teaching French, there were two French teachers, and Betty
Vacani came to take dancing classes. Kate began humbly as a nursery
helper, handling the four- and five-year-olds, "washing their hands,
sharpening their pencils, taking them for walks, playing the piano for
their nursery rhymes", as Lady Eden has said. The nursery classroom
was a sunny modern annexe built in the garden, into which games
and kindergarten lessons spilled on sunny days. It was a happy,
well-knit staff and Kate readily made friends, inviting them home to
the flat she shared for a time with another girl. Among these
colleagues, one now notes with interest, was another fair-haired
Yorkshire girl, three or four years her senior, Lavinia Keppel, who
had joined Lady Eden's the previous year. Miss Keppel remained for
some fifteen years before she took up private teaching and in 1968
was subsequently appointed by the Queen as governess at
Buckingham Palace to Prince Edward and his small class of friends—
including, by pleasant circumstances, none other than the Duchess of
Kent's nephew, James Ogilvy . . .

Most of the children lunched at school, "only the best English
meat and fresh vegetables, nothing frozen", as Lady Eden insisted.
This was Kate's first experience of the disciplines of nine till five, five
days a week, with Saturday mornings taken up with hair-dressing
and shopping. When her youngest brother John and Carolyn
Hardinge announced their engagement, she had to buy the wedding
gift at the height of the Christmas rush, and Christmas itself saw a
rush of preparation for a delectable adventure, for the wedding was
to take place in Christ Church Cathedral, Montreal, on the third
Saturday in January, with Katharine as a bridesmaid.

Carolyn's father, Viscount Hardinge, is one of the most remarkable
figures in Canadian business life, a member of the London, Montreal
and Toronto Stock Exchange, with financial interests ranging from

banking and insurance to hotels and Jamaican public transport. A
cousin of the Nevills, those close friends of the Queen, he also met
and married his Ottawa wife while serving as A.D.C. to the
Governor General of Canada at Rideau Hall and was delighted that
his elder daughter was to resume the marriage ties with England.
Katharine and her mother flew over for the wedding and, in Ottawa
itself, the genial Hardinges had taken over whole floors of the
Ritz-Carlton hotel and whirled their guests on a round of parties,
celebrations and sumptuous sight-seeing. Katharine was a charming
bridesmaid in a crinoline frock of white grosgrain, with a muff, Juliet
cap and ballerina slippers in crimson velvet. Yet she walked into her
classroom as usual, fresh and rested, as if it had all been a dream, on
the first day of term.

But change was indeed in the air, never demonstrated more
dramatically than when Kate went home to Hovingham Hall for the
mid-term weekend to find that the horrific statue of Samson Slaying
the Philistine had at last disappeared from the Samson Hall, creating
in its absence after two and a half centuries extraordinary new effects
of space and sunlight and beauty. It would indeed in future be an
atmosphere of love, not war, a decidedly apt change in domestic
detail when John and Carolyn arrived at Easter from Paris, where
they had spent part of their honeymoon. It might be added that the
Metropolitan Museum of New York had steadily offered ever larger
sums for the much-coveted and admired example of Giovanni
Bologna, and the soaring value had almost kept step with the
younger Worsleys' dislike of their superb but highly unsuitable
mascot. When the Victoria and Albert Museum offered £25,000, Sir
William Worsley could no longer resist. The sum seemed larger
then than now, a small fortune which perhaps helped to launch John
in his own entirely successful business ventures in Canada. At all
events, Samson now frienziedly slays the anguished Philistine at
South Kensington, thoughtfully placed in a vaulted hall, curiously
akin to its former setting.

Katharine had come of age, celebrating her twenty-first birthday as
just another working day at school, and perhaps she confided to John
that she had enjoyed her London year but intended to come home
that summer. Their mother had not been particularly well: Lady

Worsley suffered from arthritis and needed help in coping, especially with the duties imposed by the Lord Lieutenancy. But, this aside, Kate felt free and grown-up, fully eager for adult responsibility, and she decided of her own accord to leave Lady Eden's that summer and return home to help her mother at Hovingham Hall.

III

A family wit once remarked that one could trace Kate's energies by the Hovingham Festivals. That early audacious effort of 1951, her first year home from Oxford was, in fact, repeated with greater success the following year. The first Festival had disappointed Kate a little by not gaining more than local recognition. John had teased her with knowing nothing of the arts of publicity and, early in 1952, a dignified yet alluring brochure appeared alike through the letterbox of the *Malton Gazette* and on the editorial desks of *The Times*.

The "enlarged programme", as it was called, was to include "operatic, orchestral and choral works", commencing—for those who could match Kate's enthusiasm—with Tudor madrigals and sixteenth century instrumental music at 11 a.m., and progressing to a performance of Purcell's *Dido and Aeneas* in the Riding School of Hovingham Hall. This was complete to an orchestra in eigtheenth century wigs, an eight-year-old Cupid, and Katharine herself in the chorus. As Lady Worsley had forecast, and as indeed she made sure, a singer mantled in the lustre of Glyndebourne came in the person of Marina de Gabarain, the Italian soprano. There was an evening concert by the Jacques Orchestra, giving Rossini, Bach and Beethoven, and the high excitement of a broadcast Sunday afternoon recital when Maria Linka, Georgina Dobree and Margaret Kitchen played Bartok's *Contrasts* and Owen Brannigan mightily delivered a group of north-country folk songs. For the first time, too, Festival events were held in neighbouring houses, and the Fathers of Ampleforth Abbey, the family of Herbert Read at Stonehouse and a section of the Leeds Philharmonic Choir were among the notable Yorkshire participants.

This was in 1952. Both in 1953 and 1954, the lapse of the Festival precisely matched Katharine's absence from home. But in 1955 Kate was back at Hovingham, and so was the Festival in new strength, its attractions spread ever wider, from Elizabethan musicians magnificently arranged in the Great Chamber of Gilling Castle to a coffee concert in the Hovingham ballroom. David Ward, the bass, came from Sadlers Wells to sing in a Monteverdi opera, and Kate trained Aunt Joyce's youngest children, Edward and Angela, who gave exemplary performances in a scene in which David played an awesome Pluto. Maria Korchinska gave a harp recital and the splendid recently discovered Hovingham harpsichord came equally into its own with a recital of seventeenth century keyboard music by Vere Pilkington.

So much for the highlights of those renewed Hovingham years. Oliver acted as concert compere, and Katharine applied her abundant nervous energies to the details of organisation. There was the mounting optimism and impetus of rehearsals, with both amateurs and professionals, and the necessary arrangements for hospitality, costume hire, scene painting, and lighting for the musicians. The school children were coached in singing "Summer is Icumen In", and even Lady Worsley was inveigled into appearing in Festival scenes. Her health had improved, but her best pick-me-up—and one of the prime family preoccupations of the year—had occurred a month or two before the Festival, when Marcus stood for Parliament as Conservative candidate for Keighley in the General Election.

To Lady Worsley it was like reliving her girlhood again, richly enjoying the excitement of the election, though from a distance, for the Lord Lieutenant and his lady are debarred from political activity. In a hard-fought three-cornered contest, Marcus lost to the Labour member by 3,403 votes. This was nevertheless the election, shortly after the resignation of Winston Churchill, when a Conservative government was returned with an increased majority under Anthony Eden and Marcus Worsley duly triumphed in a straight fight at Keighley in the next General Election. "If at first you don't beat them," he echoed his mother, "you must try, try again . . ."

Yet his 1955 defeat was also shadowed by family tragedy. Lady Colegate had been seriously ill for some time; perhaps the gravity of her illness had been kept from Katharine but, the month before the election, she had to be told that her aunt had died. This was the favourite Aunt Winifred whom we have seen at Katharine's birth and christening, an affectionate figure at so many family reunions, not least the summer holiday of Coronation year at her home on the Isle of Wight. "Such fun" Kate had said, "to have to take a boat to get home!"

Katharine's sorrow, the first of her adult life, was not readily laid aside. But the Festival preoccupied her and, in family life, happiness so often follows the darker clouds. Later that year, Marcus was victorious on a gentler battleground. His engagement was announced to Bridget Assheton, daughter of Lord Clitheroe, and Katherine was one of the five bridesmaids at the country wedding at St Leonard's, Downham, with Oliver as best man.

The wedding was only two weeks before Christmas, and the bridesmaids' ensemble was seasonable, in long gowns of red velvet, with head-dresses and sprays of guelder roses and Christmas roses, in contrast to the bride's own parchment crinoline gown. Katharine seems a shy and enchanting figure in a wedding group taken at Downham Hall. "You will be next," they teased her, accurately, as it chanced. And yet, at twenty-two, she conspicuously had no boy friends on hand. Sociable, popular, she tended to treat most young men as she treated her brothers, blending raillery and rivalry, and no one knew that she would meet the Duke of Kent within the year.

At Hovingham Hall, she could lapse happily into the homebody, picking up cookery tips from Mrs Hackett, the cook; shampooing her own hair, helping her mother in the garden, making her usual round of old friends. On Sundays she played the organ in church; slipping behind the curtain ahead of the first worshippers; occasionally playing at weddings and christenings. The organ pipes, richly blazoned in blue, old rose and gold, a Festival inspiration, seldom failed in intrinsic solace, and if she sometimes slipped away from home a trifle moodily she could plead organ practice.

To the village, "Miss Katharine" was always cheerful, "unspoiled", as they said, unstuffy, smiling, extrovert. When going into York for shopping, she would sometimes enquire, "Is there anything I can get?" and so execute a dozen little commissions. An old man of ninety named Roger Bowes used to watch for her from the window of his brookside cottage, so great was his pleasure in seeing her, and if he happened to be at the back of the house when she passed, she would rap on window or door and wait to exchange a word, talking of people and weather and aches or pains.

In 1955 and again in the following year, Katharine and Oliver indulged in the first joint birthday celebrations they had enjoyed since Oxford, and the Hall was lively all the day long with visitors, culminating in a dance that evening. "I'm nearing the end of my twenties," said Oliver with mock despondency, "Katharine still a baby—at the beginning!" Upstairs, in the Ionic Hall, converted into a cinema, Sir William showed the films he had once made of his children, acting in little plays, movies now greeted with gales of laughter. Hovingham Hall had never been more crowded, for the Worsleys of course knew all the local people, all the "county", as they say. At that time, a young photographer named Antony Armstrong-Jones was still taking society photographs and if he had not moved on from mere social gossip photographs, he could have had a field day, photographing the Ropners of Bedale, the Legards and Dawnays of Malton, the Aykroyds of Wetherby, the Clutterbucks of Hornby Castle, the Howe-Herricks of Clifton Castle, the Lumleys and Lawsons and Digby Lawsons and all the others of that tight-knit North Riding social set who came to the dance.

But to "the birthday girl and boy" their younger guests were, of course, friends they had known since childhood. The entertaining at Hovingham Hall was rather more staid at times. Sir William Worsley's guest-book as Lord Lieutenant included magistrates and judges, aldermen and mayors, officers from Catterick, charity organizers, municipal and county officials and so forth. Katharine was unaware of her implicit training for future tasks when she helped her parents entertain the Lord Mayor of York to lunch or welcomed circuit judges, bishops and deans, officials of Leeds University, chief constables, charity organizers and all the others whom her father entertained—in a sense as proxy for the Queen—in his role as Lord Lieutenant. The Princess Royal is remembered, in the course of an official visit to Filey, talking to her mother, of music festivals and Harewood litter louts, "I had to go round the garden picking up bottles". But the Princess was also an old friend and neighbour; her younger son, Gerald Lascelles, had been at Eton with Marcus, and amid all the circumstances that led to the marriage of the Duke of Kent and Katharine Worsley, the Princess Royal's own marriage into a Yorkshire family in 1922 can be seen as a primary thread in the fabric.

There is a family story that in the summer of 1956, Sir William casually remarked at the dinner-table that the Duke of Kent was being posted to Catterick and Kate's only response, it is said, was a disinterested, "What regiment's he in?" In fact, the Duke was still only twenty, and Katharine knew little more of him than any other casual newspaper reader: that he was bent on an Army career and had successfully graduated from Sandhurst.

He had, in reality, passed 44th out of 220 and had won the Grierson prize for modern languages—and Katharine knew that he enjoyed dancing and was hazardously fond of fast cars. There remained little else to know except the newspaper gossip, most of which was patently absurd. In the 1950's, alas, in the wake of the Townsend affair, the "popular" gossip columnists were often inclined to write of royalty with pens dipped in amalgam of hysteria, exaggeration and even malice, and the young Duke fell a frequent victim to the snide headline, the unforeseen photoflash, and such tactics as the rumour which would be "corrected" only to cause deeper rumour. If an unwary Mama announced that she was giving a dance for her daughter, and if the Duke was a guest, the daughter was promptly dubbed "a girl friend" and the embarrassed "playboy Duke" found the names of his dancing partners mercilessly reiterated in cold and congealing print.

Happily, Katharine read very little of this sad stuff. If juvenile clowning photographs of the Duke at winter sports appeared in a newspaper, she would have turned the page with little interest. Events at Hovingham Hall did not move to the columnists' tempo. The yew alleys were clipped, the late roses plucked, the painted cricket-score signs stacked away in the pavilion. In September, when the Royal Scots Greys was transferred to Catterick as a training unit, Sir William entertained, and was entertained by, the high brass of the regiment. And so, one Sunday in late October, it came about there was a luncheon party of about ten people at Hovingham Hall, with four young officers, including the Duke and his adjutant, Captain J. C. Walton, and a family group that included Katharine and, so far as one can recollect, her "Aunt Joyce", Mrs Edward Worsley. With its pale pine coloured walls and gleaming Chippendale and Hepplewhite furniture, the dining-room at Hovingham is a pleasant apartment, and it proved a lively and congenial meal.

Prince Edward, as he was being styled, was taller than Katharine expected, broader-shouldered and more sun-tanned, with a deep attractive voice, readily breaking into laughter. Only a week or two earlier, he had celebrated his coming-of-age with a party at Coppins which the Queen and Prince Philip attended, and he told with rueful good humour how a girl reporter had been found in the house, running the wrong way down a corridor. Katharine and the Duke discovered that they had a mutual acquaintance in Mrs Oliver Millar, the wife of the deputy Surveyor of the Queen's Pictures, formerly Delia Dawnay, a Malton girl who had been a school friend of Katharine's at Castle Howard. After lunch, when the conversation turned to art, Lady Worsley showed the Duke round some of the family pictures, and he paused admiringly at the portrait of the daughter of the house painted by Sir Timothy Eden, and then turned to Katharine with a boyish grin. "But it doesn't do you justice, Miss Worsley," he said.

6 Man and Maid

If love ye virgin's heart invade,
How like a moth the simple maid...

John Gay, *The Beggar's Opera*
(The December chimes)

I

One of the private dilemmas of royalty continually crops up in the difficulty of returning hospitality. The Princess Royal was, however, a helpful and understanding aunt during the Duke of Kent's two years at Catterick, and one of her "little lunches" at Harewood House was staged with her nephew in mind early in his Worsley acquaintance. As another prelude of friendship, there stands nearly opposite Hovingham Hall, the pleasant Georgian range of the Worsley Arms Hotel, developed by the first baronet under the early Victorian ambition to fashion Hovingham into a spa, and it may be true that the Duke once youthfully proposed an incognito dinner at the Arms, only to be persuaded to dine at the Hall instead. On one such occasion, early in 1957, Katharine charmed the Prince by playing some Mozart and Beethoven after dinner and her zeal for the Hovingham festivals was equated by his own zest for Bayreuth, which he had visited as a Wagner enthusiast a year or two earlier.

It would be rash to attempt to chart the chronology of romance with precision. The two young people themselves could scarcely tell how acquaintance grew so swiftly into friendship, or how that first mutual sympathy deepened into the magnetism of love. The social ease of first names—"Please call me Edward" and her reciprocal "Katharine!"—was merely a latchpin of affection. Young "Lieutenant Kent" early discovered Kate's unwavering discretion. One could talk with candour and she responded with quick understanding; she had always liked talking to people but could be trusted

Winter and Summer—two delightful family photographs of Katharine Worsley as a child. (*Cathcart Archives*)

Hovingham Hall

The Tapestry Hall. (*Country Life*)

The Worsley family group, 1960. Standing at back, left to right, Katharine, John, Oliver. Seated, left to right, Marcus, Sir William Worsley, Lady Worsley, Mrs. Marcus Worsley and her children, Sarah and William, Mrs. John Worsley and her son, Henry, and (foreground) Willa

The Duke of Kent and Katharine at Hovingham, shortly after their engagement. (*Press Association*)

the balcony of the Mansion House, waving to
y crowds, 1961. (*Press Association*)

The bride and groom, York Minster, June 8th, 1961.
(*Keystone*)

e wedded pair pose at Hovingham Hall,
udy by Cecil Beaton. (*Camera Press*)

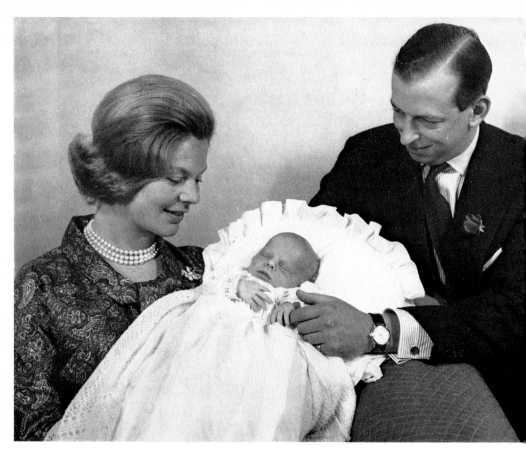

The proud parents shortly after the birth of their son
George (Earl of St. Andrews), 1962. (*Press Association*)

never to pass things on, let alone betray a confidence. At one of their early meetings, a private dance given by Mrs Howard Aykroyd at Stockeld Park, it was seen that they were "finding a lot to talk about, as well as dancing" and another friend said that they had winter sports, music, riding and country life in common, "good enough to be going on with".

It should be mentioned, however, that other Yorkshire roses similarly won smiles and attention: Valerie Lawson, daughter of Sir Ralph Lawson, Carol Pease of Sledwich Hall and Julia Williamson of Bilborough Manor, all these found their names in the newspapers chiefly on the strength of attending the same dances or house-parties as the young Duke of Kent. A fair proportion of the girls of this social belt had been school friends of Princess Alexandra at Heathfield, a link even more marked in London where some of the sophisticates whom the Duke brought home to Coppins somewhat alarmed Princess Marina and even alarmed Prince Edward himself, assessing them against his sister's own natural candour and high sense of values. In contrast, Katharine was unspoiled, young for her age, "a giggly little girl", even naive, according to one friend: the difference was between orchids from behind the plateglass of a Mayfair florist and the springtime garden flowers that decked Hovingham Hall.

Significantly, one of the Duke's favourite photographs, which the present author was shown that summer, depicted Katharine in a white summer frock, seated on the ground under a great Hovingham beech, her arms full of roses, her little black poodle, Charles, beside her, a Watteau idyll. The Duke's letters home soon suggested that Catterick was not all barrack-square discipline, and his preferences grew more evident when he began skipping weekend leave at home in favour of Yorkshire pleasures.

To be definitive, there was the Bedale Hunt fancy-dress ball, for which the Duke borrowed a Tudor costume of crimson doublet and hose, with a broad-brimmed feathered hat, and arrived, masked, with Kate as a Dresden shepherdess in bonnet and shawl. With some slight exaggeration, they can be said to have danced every dance together and it was not until the small hours that the tall Tudor drove his Dresden figurine safely home. Meanwhile, they gleefully discovered that they had both bought gramophone records at the same little

Kensington shops; they knew some of the same pleasant restaurants and had enjoyed exploring the same Kensington lanes. Edward readily talked about his brother, Prince Michael, who was fourteen and at Eton, and Katharine's interest was genuine, for brothers had always filled the horizons of her world.

With two days' leave, the Duke spent part of the Easter weekend at Hovingham. It was an occasion of April showers and an opportunity for exploring the house. The grandfather clock on the stairs is fronted with a door and spandrels of bevelled mirror, reflecting all who pass, and never, surely, such a promising young couple as Edward and Kate, their faces flushed with the sheer pleasure of one another's company. They tried out the wonderful harpsichord in the ballroom; they stepped into the gallery to look down at the Duke's parked sports car in the Riding School—he then had a Sunbeam Rapier—and were convinced that no more elegant or alluring equipage had ever been seen there. They toured the pictures "rather thoroughly": there are some good Primitives and Dutch paintings, a Rubens sketch or two, and Edward was amused by a landscape of Hampton Court, with a coach in the foreground in which Oliver Cromwell is unmistakably the passenger.

If the Duke smiled, at another point, when Kate invited him to look at the watercolours, she was guileless. A series of small service rooms had recently been converted into a gallery for her parents' collection. There were Rowlandsons, Girtins and Cotmans, as well as contemporary drawings by John Piper and others. The Duke was knowledgeable; some of the drawings could have been interchangeable with others familiar to him all his life at Coppins . . . and he was an entertaining companion to show around.

For Katharine, probably the most unexpected discovery was that Prince Edward was lonely, outwardly gregarious and a good mixer and yet solitary, with a growing troubled awareness of royal segregation akin to her own feminine sense of isolation as the one girl in a family of boys. She was attracted by the outer dignity the impress, that came of being royal, and within this aura she found the urbanity and thoughtfulness of the man he was truly becoming. The Duke of Kent, Prince Michael and Princess Alexandra are, in fact, the only British-born members of the present Royal Family whom we find to be descended on both sides from emperors and kings. On his father's side, the Duke of Kent's ancestry can be traced back for thirty generations to the King Harold who fell at the Battle of Hastings, as well as to William the Conqueror. On his mother's side, he descends from the Czar Nicholas I of Russia, not to mention Charlemagne, if you wish, or the innumerable historic links through the Danish and Greek royal families.

Princess Marina never ceased to impress their lineage upon her children. "Breeding will out," she would say, as an unshakeable and foremost tenet of family life. Edward shrugged his shoulders, with more than his own share of an accompanying family trait of self-mockery. Autographing the dance-band drum in a night-club, he pencilled defiantly, "They can't hang me for it!" But Edward had his own private sense of royal values, with duty foremost among them. It was many months, too, before Katharine could relax in her own subtle sense of royal dignity. She noticed that intimates often addressed him as "Eddie" but she continued to call him "Edward" until he bade her otherwise. And she would blithely say, "Come on, Edward, we shall be late!" while others waited upon his unpunc-tuality. Katharine, in any case, was never too punctual herself.

II

The Duke of Kent thoroughly enjoyed the milieu of Hovingham Hall. To him it was homely, the white paint a little rainworn on the window-sills or scuffed slightly in the doorways, as at Coppins in those days, neither pristine or palatial, although he might have found it difficult to analyse the ingredients of his sense of comfort. This, too, was his familiar background: family portraits, chintz-covered armchairs and well-filled bookcases, good old furniture, some fine pieces half covered with framed photographs and the magazines and clutter of everyday. He felt at home with Katharine's parents and one May afternoon, went with Sir William to watch the West Indian cricketers at Headingley. Then the happiness of Easter at Hovingham was balanced by an invitation to Katharine to spend Whitsun at

Coppins, and Eddie gleefully drove her down, the Sunbeam Talbot lapping up the miles.

The Duke was confident, relaxed and assured at the wheel, and Katharine was never more intrinsically happy, more aware of contentment, than beside him in the car, talking, singing, lulled or watchful. They lunched at a place on the road Eddie knew where he passed apparently unrecognized, a young Army officer with a fast car and a pretty girl and, as his companion, Katharine could share and understand his relaxed sense of anonymity.

That Whitsun weekend, curiously enough, marriage was in the air, in the family atmosphere. Prince Philip's niece, Princess Margarita of Baden, was marrying Prince "Tommy" of Yugoslavia, brother of the exiled King Peter, and Eddie apologized that his sister had flown off with Philip to Germany for the wedding and would not be returning until the Sunday. Perhaps the quiet weekend, in Edward's view, would help Katharine to get to know his mother all the better. If talk of the wedding helped to pass the journey, Kate must have felt that she could never thoroughly understand all the family connections. Prince "Tommy" was only a cousin by marriage, in that his uncle, Prince Paul, was married to Edward's aunt, Princess Olga. It was all very confusing, like the meshwork of roads to Coppins itself.

Approaching from the north, Katharine was aware of skirting the west London suburbs but they turned suddenly off the road into a short length of rutted lane, and the innumerable gables and chimneys, the slightly shabby stucco and brick of Coppins undoubtedly took her by surprise. Eddie tootled his horn, the unmistakable smiling figure of the Duchess of Kent (Princess Marina) appeared at a garden door and, as Katharine said years later, "I didn't have time to breathe: I was part of the family before I knew it". She had time to no more than sketch a curtsey before a beaming teen-age schoolboy joined them. This was Prince Michael. The admiration of the two brothers for their mother was obvious and Kate had probably not anticipated someone looking quite so young or so vivaciously attractive. Nor had she expected the endearing slightly foreign intonation of Princess Marina's manner of speech. Until that very moment, she had never given a shadow of thought to the concept that, by parentage, Eddie was in reality half-foreign. And Princess Marina for her part found

Kate "a very nice girl, very nice, very English", evidently at that juncture discerning nothing more than just another of the nice girls whom her son liked at times to bring home.

Such at least was the meeting of the past Duchess of Kent and the future Duchess of Kent, of mother and daughter-in-law, recollected, perhaps a little deceptively, after the passage of time. Eddie had found Hovingham a homely reflection of Coppins, and Kate evidently found Coppins an equally likeable family home with a strong Paris accent. At Coppins one stepped direct on to the lawns through huge French windows; the whole ground floor seemed to be of large sun-lit glass doors: at Hovingham one entered the secluded gardens very deliberately after descending stairs through the Tapestry Room or by the rose-garden steps off the study. Eddie had told Kate that his mother lived in a colony of old friends: the aged Baroness de Stoeckl and her grown-up family, the Poklewska-Koziells, lived in a cottage in the grounds. Various people came in for tea. They all talked, laughed and smoked constantly: the Duchess of Kent particularly chain-smoked her own favourite brand of Turkish cigarettes. The busts of Roman emperors and of late eighteenth century notables gazed rather chillingly on the sociabilities of Hovingham. At Coppins there seemed always a twinkle of Fabergé, the inviting gleam of porcelain or the snap of gold and enamel cigarette boxes.

Changing in her room for dinner, Kate evidently tried to sort out her first impressions; she could only tell a friend afterwards of looking out at the lawns in the evening sun, so wide and fresh and airy, invitingly different indeed from yew-enclosed Hovingham.

And just as her elder brothers had introduced her to the widely different worlds that they knew in Oxford and London, so Eddie that weekend introduced her into the world of royalty with surprising completeness. It was as if he had come to understand Kate's world and was deeply anxious for her quickly to come to understand his. On the Saturday, he mentioned casually that "Aunt Elizabeth" had invited them to tea and, although they had talked of his relatives in this way before, this time it no doubt took Kate a moment or two before "the penny dropped" and she realized that Aunt Elizabeth was Queen Elizabeth, the Queen Mother.

A saluting porter, in cockaded royal hat, opened the gate for

Eddie's car at Royal Lodge. People walking about in Windsor Great Park had peered into the car to glimpse its passengers, Katharine's first experience of that particular facet of public behaviour. And then Eddie shot down the drive through a blaze of rhododendrons into the quiet sanctuary of an inner forecourt, and the door of the rather large rose-washed house opened at their approach. The inner hall, small and square, provided an anti-climax, furnished chiefly as a flower-decked stable for two rather worn rocking-horses.

The Duke must have smiled at Kate's surprise, and took her hand to introduce her into the sitting-room and present her to its well-known chatelaine. There were several other people and she was engulfed once again in friendliness. The conversation was general, ranging from some forthcoming travel to what were then the Rhodesias to talk of Yorkshire, Castle Howard, the Epsom races, gardens and the rhododendrons that could be seen glimmering far across the lawn. And presently the Queen Mother motioned Katharine to come and sit and talk at her side.

"I hear you went to school at West Runton," her Majesty said.

Katherine shyly replied that "it was ages ago".

"I know it well," said the Queen Mother, in her hesitant way. "My eldest brother . . . once lived there . . . at the Old Hall . . . perhaps you know it? The King and I . . . often visited there . . . before we were married. We used to picnic . . . at Blakeney Point. It's a very small world, don't you think? I remember the school perfectly . . ." Kate was astonished. The coincidence established an immediate bond, and yet the link was stronger and stranger than either imagined, for Lord Glamis had rented Runton Old Hall for only a year or two and it was in the drawing-room at the Hall, some ten years before his tenancy, that Miss Harcourt's aunt and uncle had listened to her plans to open a school and had offered to lend her the money to buy Runton Hall.

III

If the Duke could have had his way, he would have sought leave to present Katharine to the Queen that same evening,

but the Queen was engaged that weekend with Prince Philip's
mother, Princesss Andrew, who was somewhat of an invalid, as
Eddie explained. Instead, Princess Alexandra returned in time for
Sunday lunch, bursting in like a breeze, and bringing with her not
only Princess Olga but also Olga's daughter, Princess Elizabeth, tall,
dark and slim, unmistakably foreign. They had enjoyed a wonderful
flight home with Philip, landing at White Waltham and wasting no
time. The luncheon party bubbled with wedding talk, and no doubt
Alexandra told Katharine afterwards how sorry she was not to have
met her when visiting Yorkshire a year or two earlier, although she
had been received by Katharine's father. The two girls took to one
another at once and found an easy footing on the common ground
of their mutual interests. Alexandra particularly wished to know
about Kate's experiences at St Stephen's children's home, and the
rewarding sequel was that the Princess herself began a hospital course
in child welfare a few months later. The weekend never flagged.

One close Worsley relative, gleaning something of Kate's adventures, ventured to voice the hope that it wouldn't go to her head.
"Don't worry," said Kate. "It won't. I promise!" One infers that she
scarcely realized how closely her heart was being besieged, although
the Duke of Kent already well knew he was deeply in love. Looking
back later, both came to agree that theirs was love at first sight,
but it evidently remained love unspoken and unconfessed at the
time.

As it chanced, they had gone to the Middleton Hunt point-to-
point together only two or three weeks earlier, and were recognized
by a reporter—or, rather, their car was detected, much to the Duke's
annoyance. He had gone to a great deal of trouble for a young man's
fad of flourishing a personal car number, without thinking how
readily it could attract unsought attention. K7 had formerly belonged
to an ancient Liverpool corporation bus. The Duke of Kent was then
also seventh in the succession, in line after Charles and Anne, Princess
Margaret, and the Duke of Gloucester and his two sons. Publicity—
and perhaps even romantic rumour—was necessarily attached to his
birthright but the young Duke was coldly determined that
Katharine, above all, should not be involved. No doubt it was due to
newspaper notoriety that he could not enter a country pub with his

Catterick brother officers without a crowd gathering, often to the point of compelling him to leave. The Army, it was said, treated him as if he were classified information, top secret grade, and even young Michael agreed that he needed to be. And so, after Whitsun, when he knew that his sister and his Aunt Elizabeth liked Katharine immensely and that his mother also welcomed her warmly and without disapproval, chivalry decided him to part with both his beloved number-plate and his car. He traded in the Sunbeam Rapier for a more anonymous deep green Aston Martin inconspicuously numbered DMF 56 and had the pleasure of noting, when driving it back from London, that no policeman saluted him as they so often had with the K7.

As an occasion of equal significance, we may now also note an official visit which the Queen and her husband paid to Yorkshire on July 10th. It devolved upon Sir William Worsley, as Lord Lieutenant of the North Riding, to receive the royal visitors on their arrival at Catterick Camp Station, and the Duke of Kent escorted the Queen during her tour of inspection. It was a day of incessant rain, "royal weather . . . our weather", as the Queen always said with a wry smile. With the downpour lashing the car windows, the Duke of Kent drove with his cousins to York and later to Harrogate, where they visited the Yorkshire Show and were introduced, as a wag said, to "Yorkshire's finest cows, some unrivalled sheep and a quantity of prize poultry". But it is certain, too, that during a private interlude that day the Duke of Kent sought leave to present one of his "personal friends, Miss Katharine Worsley". He knew that his ever-helpful and sympathetic aunt at Royal Lodge would have put the Queen in the picture, and the Queen and Prince Philip in turn, smiling and kindly, though noncommittal, could tell from Eddie's glowing eagerness that this was no ordinary presentation.

The following month, indeed, when the Queen went to Balmoral and the Kents left for their usual visit to Italy and stayed with Princess Olga at the Villa Demidoff near Florence, Eddie flew home within two weeks, unwilling to spend another day of his precious leave without Katharine's company. On September 7th, Sir Leonard and Lady Ropner were giving a dance for their daughter, Merle, at Thorp Perrow, Bedale. Sir William and Lady Worsley and

Katharine were invited and, apologizing on the phone for her husband's absence, Lady Worsley mentioned diplomatically, "We may have a young house guest ... may we perhaps bring him along?" She imagined that Lady Ropner gathered her meaning: the Duke had been to dances at Thorp Perrow before. But his visits to Hovingham were now so inconspicuous that his arrival at the dance with Katharine and her mother proved a pleasant surprise.

One Saturday, he rang up to report dolefully that his car was in dock but he hoped to reach Hovingham by getting a lift. This proved to be wild optimism; an Army car dropped him at Thirsk more than twenty miles away and he travelled the rest of the way on the local bus, unnoticed by the farmers and shopping housewives, but instantly detected at the Hovingham bus-stop. Yet the Hovingham folk remained sturdily loyal to the Hall, and no whisper of this visit leaked out until his engagement to Katharine more than three years afterwards.

Thus the course of true love, young love, ran smooth, except for the acknowledged difficulty that Princess Marina regarded Eddie as too youthful to know his own mind. He diligently concentrated on his Army career, shirking nothing, but never failed to make the most of any respite that allowed him an hour or two with Katharine. Thus he sped over one evening from Catterick to take her to the little Malton cinema to see Noel Coward's naval film "In Which We Serve", and was no doubt the star's only family friend in the audience. On leave in London in October, he celebrated his twenty-second birthday with three days' dancing, attending a Belgrave Square dance on the 9th, holding his own private party on the 10th and attending a private Knightsbridge dance the following evening. The record of social engagements made no mention of Kate but, in fact, three days of unsustained bachelor merriment had become unthinkable. A boy-and-girl affair it might yet prove to be, but benevolent and godmotherly hostesses planned for "the two Kays" (Katharine and Kent) as they might plan for any other silly young bewitched couple at house-parties and dances.

It has been said that the Duke fell in love with Katharine "in the deep and single-minded fashion of his Romanov grand-uncles". He had fallen in love, too, with all the passion and certainty of his

Hanoverian ancestors, precisely as his own parents had done soon
after their first meeting. Katharine had not been present at the Duke's
coming-of-age party at Coppins in 1956, shortly before his all-
important first visit to Hovingham. But she was very definitely at
Princess Alexandra's coming-of-age party at Coppins on January 6th,
1958, another turning point in their romance. The Princess was, of
course, a Christmas Day baby, but the celebrations were held for
convenience in the New Year, and at the birthday girl's insistence,
Kate was a guest at the family dinner-party held beforehand. The
Queen and Prince Philip specially travelled up from Sandringham for
the event; Princess Margaret, to her disgust, had to remain at home
with a chill, but the Queen Mother came, Eddie's uncle and aunt
(Prince Paul and Princess Olga of Yugoslavia) were there and innumerable continental cousins. The Duke of Edinburgh opened the
dancing with Princess Alexandra; the Duke of Kent danced first with
his mother and then with the Queen and his aunt and then, duty
done, with Kate . . . and with Kate again.

Katharine knew them all now: the special friends, such as the
Herberts and Hamiltons, O'Neils and Ogilvys, Abel-Smiths and
Bowaters. A group of young officers, whom she also knew well, had
come from Catterick, their arrival a signal for comic noses, explod-
ing flowers, and a fusillade of practical jokes. Not neglecting his
duties as host, Eddie capered away to take photographs, and Angus
Ogilvy was a ready partner. In that sparkling, happy, ever-changing
evening, Katharine was still new enough to it all to enjoy a tinge of
dreamy unreality as she danced with Prince Philip or found herself
enjoyably chatting to the Queen and Queen Mother. It was still not
fifteen months since she had first met Eddie, fifteen months that had
changed her life.

IV

As if poised already between two worlds, on a springboard between
her past and her future, Katharine in 1958 celebrated her twenty-fifth
birthday both at Hovingham and at Coppins. She opened her cards
and gifts at home, not least a wonderful present from Eddie, the first

of two that day. The morning was enlivened by an anniversary visit from Aunt Joyce, with her two small daughters carrying posies; and then Oliver, blithely celebrating his own thirty-first birthday, drove her to York for the train to London. Whether they then travelled south together and were both guests at Coppins one does not know: many such embellishments are lost in diffident recollection or family reticence. It would embroider the story if they left the train at Hitchin or Hatfield to meet a motherly and friendly lady with her car and chauffeur who was also en route to Coppins, bypassing London. Eddie was in fact a genius at organising such details, and Mary, Duchess of Devonshire, had been staying with her brother, the Marquess of Salisbury, at Hatfield House. A girlhood friend of the Queen Mother, and Mistress of the Robes to the Queen, she was to prove a good and wise friend and counsellor to Kate, offering open hospitality at her house in Cheyne Walk.

Early in 1958, indeed, a series of invitations waved a wand of apparent coincidence whenever Eddie, too, was also within reach of London. That February, he was in fact taking a six-weeks riding instruction course at Aldershot, and the two young people made the best of their romantic opportunities, going to theatres or dining together in the current favourite among the intimate little candle-lit restaurants in which Chelsea abounds. One evening, Eddie took her to Clarence House for the first time, and thus Katharine first met Princess Margaret. In studying the fine tracery of royal match-making, one notices that the Duchess of Devonshire's daughter, Lady Elizabeth Cavendish, was also lady in waiting to Princess Margaret at this time, in rota with Iris Peake, and highly industrious in smoothing each new stage of the Princess's friendship with a certain Mr Antony Armstrong-Jones, today's Lord Snowdon.

If Mary, Duchess of Devonshire, should ever write her memoirs, we might in fact see the wheels in action. The dowager Duchess and the Queen Mother are nearly of the same age; both were sadly widowed within two years of one another, and both were sensible enough to assuage their sorrow by turning with maternal interest to the affairs of the young. Katharine, as we know, acutely reminded the Queen Mother of the days when she was herself merely Elizabeth Bowes-Lyon, meeting her future husband at Runton and faced with the surging dilemma of all that marriage into the Royal Family would entail. No doubt she also recognized in Katharine the potential raw material of the monarchy, the human virtues that must refresh each royal marriage close to the Throne if the system is to survive. One of Princess Marina's continental relatives maintained through every family discussion that Eddie and Kate were so right for one another, "like two sides of a coin". Marina admittedly found it difficult to adjust to the view that neither of her two elder children would marry into other royal houses and, after all, only three years had passed since her nephew, Olga's son, Prince Alexander of Yugoslavia, had married Princess Maria Pia of Savoy, eldest daughter of the ex-King Umberto of Italy. Yet Princess Alexandra had obviously fallen in love with Angus Ogilvy, and Edward made it clear in word and deed that for him there was now no one but Katharine.

Meanwhile, the Queen Mother deftly urged the young people's suit but agreed equally with Marina that there was plenty of time. "She is a pretty, sweet person", Marina agreed when describing Katharine in one of her letters. But the young people needed elder friends and closest family all around them, in the *dramatis personae* of their play, and the idyll continued to unfold happily when the scene moved again to Yorkshire.

The Duke of Kent learned with some chagrin that the newspaper gremlins were again following him and again obviously watching Kate, as if their restaurant tete-a-tetes had been noticed in London. Sir William Worsley was waylaid on the telephone and attempted to put an interrogator off the scent by agreeing that, yes, his daughter was very preoccupied with plans . . . plans for another Hovingham Festival in a year's time. But perhaps more than anyone else at Hovingham, Aunt Joyce—Sir William's sister-in-law, Mrs Edward Worsley—was in every way Katharine's ally, and no doubt delighted in her own role as conspirator whenever the love-story threatened to tilt into a comedy of secret entrances and half-serious disguises.

On days when the Duke seemed likely to have a leave-pass from Catterick, reporters could readily watch the great riding-school doors of Hovingham Hall. Indeed, they could watch in comfort, with a mug of beer in their hands, at the Malt Shovel Inn across the green. Village gossip, no matter how loyal, could no longer avoid the spread of news about the Duke's visits. But however keen and continuous the watch on Hovingham Hall, however disconcerting the questions at the Malt Shovel or the Worsley Arms, no one watched in the village of Cawton, two miles north of Hovingham and a mile or so down a side-road. The Duke's Aston Martin could always out-distance pursuers in Catterick and there were no alien eyes when his car turned into the farmyard past the barns to Aunt Joyce's home, Cawton Hall. The Hall itself, a smallish Victorian house, stands further secluded from observation on a grassy knoll beyond the farmyard, and but a mile east of Hovingham by the bridleways.

On foot, or occasionally riding one of the horses, as the spirit took her, Katharine could set out to a meeting unobserved, across the fields or down through Hovingham High Wood or along a farm track to her Aunt Joyce's door. The woods slope down to Cawton, the fields are flat and not particularly inviting to intruders. And yet it was here, walking through the kale and cabbages, that Katharine and Edward came to an understanding, perhaps "proposing to one another" as a friend said. There is equally the well-founded story that one day it came on to rain and that Edward, concerned with Katharine's hairdo, suggested they should run for shelter. Any London deb would have scampered but Kate merely laughed and took her time, the rain itself an element in courtship, as so often in Yorkshire.

At all events, Edward soon knew, as Kate had always known, every stick and stone of that beloved path, the tiny coppice halfway and the point where the wood-lark could best be heard, high above, drenching the sky with song. Oddly enough, the lonely farm road had once been full of people, even busy with a traffic of horses and carriages. More than a hundred years ago, this had been the nucleus of Hovingham Spa. The old bath-house, a charming essay in late Georgian Gothic, still stood, empty, mysterious and inviting, in a dense thicket of weeds. With its high eaves, scrolled barge-boards and delicious diamond-paned windows, Kate had breathlessly discovered, it was quite like the drawings of the original Royal Lodge, and the two sweethearts could not help but see how it might one day be renovated and converted into a delightful summer home.

Nor had it subsided too deeply into ruin. A family had occupied it as recently as the war, when every country cottage, in no matter what disrepair, offered sanctuary from bombing. As young people will, dreaming their future dreams, Eddie and Katharine pushed open a door. The rooms were damp, chill and cobwebby but there was a view through the dusty windows of what might be a lawn and the dismantled bath-hall itself could make a saloon. It stood on Worsley land and Eddie talked to Aunt Joyce excitedly about all the possibilities that bygone Worsleys had evidently overlooked. To his mother, too, he talked firmly but tactfully of his wish to marry and settle down. And then suddenly events gave new shape to his impatience. At the end of May, he came rushing over to Hovingham and Kate knew at once there was direst news. In October the Royal Scots Greys were to be transferred to Germany for two years. This had been heard of before but never with the concrete force of firm timing. Eddie would of course be going with them, and indeed he would have willingly faced no other alternative and yet the prospect of two years so far from Katharine seemed unendurable.

Older folk in their well-meaning way had always urged that there need be no haste to wed, but the regimental plans seemed to Eddie to indicate the very reverse, and within twenty-four hours, he produced a romantic solution. They could marry in Hovingham Church, as Kate would wish, and settle together into married quarters in Germany to start married life in the mood of a two-year honeymoon. Katharine was swept up despite herself into his enraptured fever, although Princess Alexandra, when hurriedly consulted on the telephone, was sympathetic but cautious. "They'll argue delay," she said, in effect. "They always do." She could obviously not say more on the 'phone. The Princess was spending the weekend with David and Myra Butter at their home in Perthshire—Myra is the younger daughter of Lady Zia Wernher—and in their mood of urgency Eddie and Katharine dashed up to see them.

The Butter's farming estate lies on the outskirts of the old town of Dunkeld, and they all went to morning service that Sunday in the parish church that was once Dunkeld Cathedral. The Butters could not be encouraging. David had not married until he was twenty-six. Eddie would not be twenty-three until October. Myra had been five years younger than her husband, while Kate was more than two years older than Edward: did that make a difference? There was, beside, the practical difficulty that Sir William and Lady Worsley were sailing to Canada in August to spend six weeks with John and his wife, Carolyn, and would not be back until early October, when the regiment would already be leaving. In the cold light of day, it became clear that the elders would indeed be daunting.

7 The Parting

Let us take the road,
Hark! I hear the sound of coaches...

Pepusch, *Lyric to Handel's March in Rinaldo*
(The March chimes)

I

On their honeymoon in 1934, the Duke of Kent's parents had met Franklin Roosevelt while he was cruising in the West Indies on Vincent Astor's yacht. As a result of this encounter, President Roosevelt became godfather eight years later to Prince Michael, and the fates may have had this fragile link in mind in 1958, when Katharine was invited on a Mediterranean cruise on Lord Astor's yacht *Delaneira*. The fates, however, were personified not in three sisters but in the Astors' other guests: Mary, Duchess of Devonshire, and her close friend, Lady Margaret Myddleton, with Lady Margaret's daughter, Fiona, who was a year or two younger than Katharine and already a close friend.

One will not be surprised to learn that Fiona was shortly to become a rota lady in waiting to Princess Margaret, so thoroughly enmeshed was Katharine now in the social web of royalty. Earlier in 1958, she had been thinking of accompanying her parents on at least part of their visit to her brother John in Toronto. Then the proposed cruise came up, as they say. Undoubtedly, the dowager Duchess of Devonshire bore in mind that the Duke of Kent would also be in the Med at that time, staying with the family as usual at Princess Olga's home in the Tuscan hills. And certainly he would be within reach of Capri and Naples where the yacht was due to dock after calling at Malta, Sicily and Sardinia.

As it turned out, the arrangements for the cruise were made before the news of his regiment's impending transfer to Germany had so deeply intensified the young Duke's impatience to wed. The holiday promised the wonderful fun of Capri and Naples, and it seemed that Katharine might then go on to the Villa Demidoff to break the agreeable news of a betrothal. As late as July, Eddie was still convinced that he could win his family over to his own way of thinking, in his eager project to waste no time before getting married. At the same time, he had no wish to upset his mother, and Princess Marina still considered him too young and inexperienced to marry and settle down.

While Kate was still cruising the Mediterranean, the issue became decisive and Eddie's holiday visit to the Villa Demidoff developed into a family conference. Prince Paul and Princess Olga both urged their mature and prudent views upon their nephew. "Your father did not marry till he was over thirty"—did this invincible argument fall into the conversation? Princess Alexandra, one suspects, tried not to take sides. Prince Michael was quite appalled at the atmosphere of fuss. Eddie's cousin, Paul and Olga's son, Prince Alexander, arrived with his wife, Princess Maria Pia "to add the counsel of his own senior ten years" and admittedly Edward's resolution was shaken.

Meanwhile, against the lively colourful kaleidoscope of all the *Delandeira's* ports of call, Katharine could half foresee the wonderful moment of meeting him and of being whisked to the villa, the private excitement of their declaration, the celebration: and instead of these rosy visions Eddie's messages to the yacht grew less hopeful. One doubts very much whether anyone mentioned the Royal Marriages Act. The previous consent of the Queen is required for the marriage of any descendant of George II until the age of twenty-five, with the alternative of twelve months notice to the Privy Council unless Parliament should meanwhile express disapproval. The Duke of Kent knew that the Queen's approval in reality depended on his mother's full approval and he had not reckoned on such emphatic and repeated advice on all sides that he should be patient. On board the yacht, the Duchess of Devonshire meantime no doubt already had news of her own and gently began explaining to Katharine the delicate and unwritten rules of royal protocol. Young couples were usually obliged to give themselves time to decide, and perhaps even to endure a measure of separation to help make sure of their affections before taking the all but irretrievable steps to the altar.

Katharine evidently knew the cause was lost before she met Eddie or shared his bleak disappointment. It came to this, that it seemed best after all that they should separate for a year and see one another as little as possible. Independently, they had each come to the same realization and, after the dismal crisis, they both reshaped their plans with happy optimism. The young, ever volatile, can make readjustments that might defeat their elders. The Duke could see how quickly two years at Catterick had flown, and the first year in Germany would surely move at equal tempo. Both Edward and Katharine were moreover aware of the element of challenge. Back in England, Kate began picking up the pieces and began to plan a 1959 Hovingham festival. Their parting, fortunately, was to commence only when the regiment left Catterick . . . and they would make the best of it.

Early in September, they were at a dance for Jean Aykroyd at Well Hall, Bedale, and some of their closest Yorkshire friends, the Legards and Ropners, noticed no dimming of gaiety, no forthcoming hint of "parting's sweet sorrow". In October, Eddie enjoyed ten days leave before he joined his unit in Germany. On October 4th, both were at the wedding in the East Riding of two of their friends, Jennifer Seed and Richard Dangar of the Queen's Royal Lancers. It was a Yorkshire country wedding at Pocklington; once again Aykroyds and Legards and Brothertons were there, and for Katharine and Edward, in the little parish church, the words of the marriage service held a private significance. Five days later, the Duke of Kent celebrated his birthday in Yorkshire with Kate without risk of publicity and in five days more, he flew out from Heathrow to Hanover.

II

One summer afternoon, the Duke had talked with interest to the two gardeners who were trimming the great yew hedge of Hovingham, watching them progressing along the vast bulk with power-driven clippers, moving their ladders along a dark-green thicket high as a house and extending farther than any street in Hovingham village. "How long does it take you?" he had asked. The men shook their heads. The job was spread over several weeks: they could never be sure. "And what happens if you don't quite finish it?" The gardeners had caught the twinkle in Kate's eye and cheerfully responded, "What we don't get done one year, we do the next!" The recollection must have comforted Kate, walking the yew alley alone in October rain. The happiness deferred from one year would come another.

She resolutely turned her thoughts to the possible new Festival programme. Eddie had made the fascinating suggestion that Handel himself might have visited Hovingham in his old age when the house was new. Katharine's research shed no light on the theory, but opened an equally attractive prospect. Why not a fantasia of Handelian airs based on the grand tour which young Thomas Worsley had surely undertaken in the eighteenth century? He may well have enjoyed a meeting with Louis XV at Versailles. As Lady Worsley said, with an eye to costume possibilities, he could have been anywhere and met anyone. Sir Herbert Read contributed to the discussion the prospect that Thomas must also have known Dr Burney, if not Fanny Burney herself. Whereupon Katharine suggested to her eldest brother, Marcus, that he might play Thomas Worsley and, surprisingly, Marcus agreed.

Aunt Joyce's children, hearing of the Festival, vociferously volunteered for *anything*, and Tommy and Susan, Angela and Diana, were agreeably cast as their ancestor Thomas Worsley's brother and sisters. Searching her operatic books, Katharine lighted on one of the sixteenth century fathers of opera, Giulio Caccini, and Herbert Read confirmed that his early opera *La Liberazione di Ruggerio* had indeed never been produced in England. Here was the opportunity for a notable premiere, and David Ward of Sadler's Wells was again booked on the strength of it, with Peter Evans as conductor of the Festival orchestra. The 1959 Festival, its organiser promised in a brochure, would follow "the original policy of combining local and international talent in programmes of new and familiar music". In the event, the Festival was held at the end of July, 1959, and turned out to be as successful as all its fore-runners. But it was chiefly Nanny Jean Thorpe and Aunt Joyce's eldest daughter, sixteen-year-old Susan, who rehearsed the three younger children, for Katharine was

then unexpectedly as far away as could be, on the other side of the
Atlantic.

A change of plan had led to this adventure, right out of the blue.
In the autumn of 1958, when Katharine so deliberately applied herself
to the festival plans, her parents returned from their visit to John and
Carolyn in Canada, laden with films and photographs. The transparencies of John's sun-browned six-months-old baby son flashed on the
screen, with pictures of their Toronto house and a cottage up at the
lakes, and of John and Carolyn and their little girl, three-year-old
Willa, splashing somewhere in a Hardinge swimming-pool. "How
wonderful!" said Kate. Lady Worsley was not insensitive to the hint
of wistfulness, and needed only to mention her daughter with
maternal solicitude in a letter to John and Carolyn. And then
delightfully, there came an airmail inviting Kate to Toronto, begging
her to come and see the children, to come as early as she could and
to stay for as long as she liked. Urging Katharine to accept, Lady
Worsley pointed out that Oliver could manage the Festival; there
was little to detain her in England. Kate looked undecided, but the
prospect of seeing her brother's babies was all too alluring and, in
mentioning his children, John had played a trump card.

Katharine found that it all happened with breathless speed. She
spent an afternoon shopping in York and, a few days later, she
boarded the midday plane at London Airport and watched the light
fading over the Quebec muskeg until the plane dropped down
through the snow clouds to the lights of Toronto glinting and
flashing in the dusk. Then she alighted to the sudden chill and cold
and the sight of John and Carolyn waving wildly from the airport
buildings, and suddenly a little girl was hoisted shoulder-high for her
first glimpse of her fair and beautiful aunt from England.

One can believe that Kate forgot everything in the joy of that
family reunion, and in the fast drive along the lake shore, amid the
busy traffic and vivid neons. "Lake Ontario!" cried John, as if it
belonged to him. "Lake Ontario, Auntie Kathrun," echoed three-
year-old Willa. The towering apartment and office blocks of the city
began slipping by, hardly noticed in the fun and wonderful excitement of everyone talking at once. The car turned into quieter
tree-lined roads where the lights of houses gleamed across the snow.

"Here we are—here's Vesta Drive," said Carolyn. Already "talking Canadian" herself, Kate might have guessed that Number 306 would be at "the next block" or beyond "the next intersection". And then she recognized the house, John's home, from the white clapboard gable and painted white mullions she had seen in the transparencies. The steps to the front door were half-covered by snow, and in a moment more, inside, in the warmth, the baby Harry was presented to her and she was holding him—delicious, delectable, a picture no longer but warm and tangible in her arms.

John had once jokingly written home that Number 306 reminded him of Yorkshire and it was in fact a pleasant house of dark brick and white windows, modern but with a pleasing touch of Victorian character, a house on a fifty-foot lot close to its neighbours in the more elite Forest Hill district of north-central Toronto and near Forest Hill village itself. On her first day, indeed, Katharine found herself being initiated into what was then exclusively the North American art of trolley-pushing in the local super-mart, and she little dreamed that within five years she would be trundling her basket just as expertly in a super-market in Hong Kong. On her first evening, she delighted in going on her knees, white-aproned, to help bathe the baby.

There was no need for Willa to stay up "for Daddy to come home and tell me a story", when her magical English aunt could promptly get her to bed and invent a story about the clowns and balloons of the nursery wallpaper. Katharine's room with its diamond-paned windows and blue shutters was a pleasant serene retreat for writing letters. Carolyn was an indulgent sister-in-law and saw that Kate had the admirable trait with children of "enjoying without spoiling". A lot of time was spent in the nursery but, as I wrote only two years later,★ Kate's happiness was relative. "Every car passing her brother's house seemed to contain a happy couple—and every couple seemed to emphasize her separation."

John could say teasingly that he was with the royal trust company—as indeed he was—but no hint of his sister's private life ever reached the scores of Canadian friends to whom he introduced

★ *Toronto Star Weekly*, 1961.

her. Katharine explored the town: the little boutiques of Bloor and
Eglinton and the apparently limitless departments of Eaton's and
Simpson's. In practical reality, it must be said that she window-
shopped a little pensively under the handicap of the £50 "travel
allowance" which was all that was then vouchsafed by a stringent
government. Window-gazing, she would sometimes find herself, as if
in a dream, confronting photographs of the Queen or the Queen
Mother. And inevitably, with a sense of alien strangeness, there must
have been considerations of whether she really wished to marry into
the Royal Family, whether life could be sufficiently free and uncon-
stricted, whether indeed she wished to become perhaps the sixth lady
of England. Yet she had never really thought of Eddie in this way. In
her self-deprecating moments, there was the much more tangible
possibility that he might meet somebody else, and John in turn was
perhaps not above mock warnings that some handsome Canadian
might sweep her off her feet.

Kate stayed in Canada only a month on this occasion and was
home at Hovingham in time for Christmas. If time in the New Year
of 1959 seemed to move on leaden wings, there are friends who
vaguely remember a winter sports holiday. Princess Alexandra wrote
regularly, though whether Edward was also free to write, under the
terms of their promise, must remain a romantic secret. But in
February there came letters with exotic Mexican postage stamps;
Alexandra and her mother were in Mexico as a prelude to their
South American tour, and the Princess's ecstatic impressions fired
Kate's imagination. She browsed over travel leaflets and one day
unfolded an astonishing fact to Fiona Myddleton. "Do you know," she
challenged with triumphant excitement, "that one can go from Canada
to Mexico City by Greyhound coach for only seventy dollars?"

III

The mere idea of travelling as far as Mexico City had suddenly
introduced a new dimension. Fiona was fully eager to join in such an
adventure; Katharine perhaps had cause to regret having lavished
part of her new travel allowance on winter sports, but she could

demonstrate a somewhat wilful Worsley independence and was sure that she could raise the necessary extra funds by taking a job in Canada for the summer. John and Carolyn hospitably proposed that both Fiona and Katharine should stay with them for the summer and plans fell into place.

Kate's travel ideas developed, indeed, into a full-dress and, to her parents, quite alarming scheme: not only to travel across Canada coast-to-coast by Greyhound coach but down the Pacific coast all the way to Mexico City, with a divergence to the Grand Canyon, and then by coach northward up the Atlantic seaboard, as near as possible, to Washington. Eager and elated, the two girls arrived in Toronto in June, and now Kate found the city in full leaf, the pavements blistering with heat, while in the Vesta Drive "back-yard", baby Harry was learning to walk barefoot on the grass.

Kate was fully determined, too, on taking a job, refusing within the integrity of her own strict rules all offers of a loan from John, and least of all to accept a gift from him. Checking time-tables, brooding deeper through travel brochures, she planned a tour rather as if she were organizing a Hovingham festival, and decided that it might be possible in three months to save up the necessary funds out of earnings.

Her first thought was to look after children, but the inconsiderable Canadian demand for teaching assistance or temporary nursery school staff made her reluctantly change her mind. Happily, John mentioned that he had a friend who might help. He happened to know a partner in Henry Birks and Sons, the foremost Toronto jewellers, and "it was all as good as arranged".

Every great city has at least one highly distinguished firm in command of the luxury trade in wedding gifts, engagement rings, anniversary and commemoration gifts, gold, silver and jewellery. One thinks of Tiffany's in New York, Cartier of Paris, Garrard, the Crown jewellers of London, and others besides. Birks have similarly long reigned supreme in Toronto, a lush, luxurious department store in miniature, as if Asprey's had been transferred across the Atlantic to settle effectively in lower Yonge Street. It has been said that her ancestors must have been sufficiently aristocratic to lose their heads in the French Revolution if a girl is to be employed at Cartier's, and the ladies of Tiffany's give the equal impression that their families, too, are desirably linked with the upper Four Hundred. There happens to be a quick turnover in the feminine staff itself in such exclusive establishments, especially during the summer and so Birks unhesitatingly accepted Miss Katharine Worsley, promptly recognizing the sales merit of such a young and pretty English blonde, poised and attractive and yet natural and charming.

Working duchesses are a commonplace nowadays but a future royal duchess has probably never before worked as a salesgirl in a store. Birks pride themselves on their English porcelain as well as their diamond clasps, on their handbags and leather as well as gold toiletry. Katharine served for a short time at each counter to gain some training experience before being assigned to the gift salon. Always a dunce in arithmetic, she found some difficulty in coping with dollars and cents. She was a "new girl" and a temporary minor assistant, but senior salesmen and one or two regular customers sometimes sought her opinion, quickly recognizing her flawless taste.

Excitedly rushing home to Vesta Drive with her first pay check, she insisted on taking John and Carolyn out to dinner. Her brother usually drove her down-town and dropped her off on the way to his office, but when a business trip took him to Montreal, she blithely explained in a letter home that she had only to walk a block to the bus. Toronto was then in the full delirium of constructing its new subway system and Kate learned her way around the morass of road works like any other city girl. One day, when walking down Yonge Street to a lunch counter, an English voice hailed her, and it was a girl whom she had known at Runton Hill School. It made a small world, indeed . . .

And then suddenly there was the faintest tinge of gold in the foliage, and with this hint of the fall, with time-tables checked and rechecked, with visas in order, it was time to be off. It was a glorious lark, buoyed by John's successful insistence at the last moment on the need of a contingency fund. The prudent had thought that the girls should fly at least as far as Winnipeg and so avoid the featureless prairies. But there was plenty of time. In one's mid-twenties, every hamlet, barn, motel or farmstead is of interest, and the lumber stacks of Sault Ste Marie, the name signs of Wawa, the grain towers of Port Arthur were as beautiful and notable as peaks in Darien.

Three days out, in Winnipeg, Katharine and Fiona already felt seasoned travellers, veterans of the quick lunch, shrewd judges of hotel facades and experts in swift sight-seeing. Yet with their arrival in Calgary and then Banff for their first week-end, with 1500 miles behind them, Kate's postcards and letters grew ecstatic. The Queen and the Duke of Edinburgh had been there some weeks earlier, and the current wisecrack was that even the grizzly bears had been washed and shampooed. Rebelling in the fantastic panorama of the scenery, the mountains and glaciers, waterfalls and lakes, Katharine little knew that she would one day watch the Queen's own cine-film of the Rockies in an amateur movie show at Windsor Castle, and one day ride through Calgary in a sort of triumph with the Duke of Kent.

On that first visit Banff was past the full tourist season, the cabin camps no longer crowded, the air crisp with autumn. Through Glacier and Rogers Pass the road and railway ran side by side, and Katharine was to find that the Queen's film, shot from the rear observation platform of her train, vividly recaptured the cliffs and screes and canyons, the grandeur of every prospect in the crystal light, totally recalling the urgency of her wish to share it all with Eddie.

Through Kamloops and Cache Creek, the Thompson and Fraser canyons, each successive name-sign posed a question-mark in her personal interrogation of her future. Vancouver is a fantasia of skyscrapers, mountains and blue water to every new arrival, but for Kate it was also the first forwarding address for mail after two weeks or more, and no letter was more eagerly anticipated than one from Princess Alexandra. Earlier in the year, the Princess had been at Goodwood motor-races with "E" during his leave and she may have hinted at only "standing-in" for Kate. With every letter, some such hint rapturously told Katharine all that she longed to know.

IV

John and Carolyn had, of course, effected introductions in Vancouver and Victoria, but the lavish hospitality of British Columbia must, as always, have astonished the travellers. They were greeted with welcoming parties, whirled here and there on sight-seeing trips and no doubt when their hosts insisted on driving them across the American border to Seattle, there were the usual Vancouver parting jokes that "the States would give them a chance to rest up". There followed three or four days of travel southward from Portland, riding through the region of giant redwoods, making leisurely coach stopovers as they pleased, and then they came to the realm of orchards and vineyards and straggling suburbs that lead at last to the Golden Gate Bridge.

And here again, in San Francisco, the long arm of Hardinge acquaintance reached out to link them with new friends, so that local folk squired them through the exuberance of Fisherman's Wharf and swept them proudly to the viewpoint of Telegraph Hill. They rode the Powell Street cable cars, and got out to help push and turn them around, too, as all tourists like to do on the single-end runs. They wandered through Chinatown and trudged along Market Street and made sure of seeing Gump's, that elite store which Katharine had heard frequently mentioned while at Birk's.

If Thomas Worsley ever kept a journal of any Grand Tour, it still awaits a finder among the uncatalogued papers at Hovingham Hall. Probably Katharine's postcards from America have long since been destroyed and travel journals have gone out of fashion. But if a 10,000-mile coach tour is a test of stamina, it also sheds many a sidelight on the traits of personality, and illustrates the sense of adventure, determination, resourcefulness and constant interest in people so apparent in today's Duchess of Kent. Never able to resist a crying baby, she must have murmured, "Please may I take him?" and soothed many a fractious child on the Greyhound routes, though such trivial episodes fade quickly from memory. Characteristically, also, Katharine had put it to Fiona that it was preferable to pass up the sights of Hollywood and Los Angeles in favour of the Grand Canyon: it is not often one can find oneself within a few hundred miles of the most astonishing natural spectacle on earth.

The bus time-tables appeared bent on cloaking the Grand Canyon in obscurity, but evidently Kate had worked out a day-long route from Santa Barbara via such staging points as Bakersfield, Williams and Flagstaff (Arizona). On every bus, others had done the same, eagerly comparing routes and schedules as part of the game of Find-the-Canyon, and when the driver from Flagstaff boomed out

"You are now entering the Grand Canyon National Park", his passengers had a glimpse of an arched gateway as if man had determined to imprison a monster within the park boundaries, and all the travellers beamed and smirked upon one another with the culminating joy and achievement of finding themselves there at last.

If it had perplexed Kate in deciding whether to reserve rooms, she was no doubt glad to have done so at first sight of the cars and coaches and people around the ranging wooden lodge that is the El Tovar hotel. Probably the two coaching companions jokingly asked the reception clerk where the Grand Canyon was, as all visitors do, and the clerk equally summed up their English accents and gave the usual British variant of the standard reply "It's the first hole you see—you can't miss it!"

"It is as if the sky had suddenly turned over and made a bowl at my feet," I noted my own impressions. "You look down and see peaks and pyramids and can hardly realize they are mountains. It is as if the Alps have been turned upside down in a chaos of angry red and purple rock." But the Canyon is similarly "a mere ditch, a river bed, violently hewn by the world's most turbulent river; and wind and storm, all the forces of erosion, are still completing the astonishing sculpturing ... One watches the Canyon fill with deep shadow as the sun sets, while the topmost peaks glow fiery crimson. Having looked at the Canyon from one point, one motors for twenty miles along the rim to Hermit's Rest to gaze down at a slightly different view of the same panorama, and one drives for miles in another direction for the view at the eighteen-miles 'widest point'." Missing nothing, Katharine would have ridden muleback via the Kaibab Trail to the bottom of the Canyon at Phantom Ranch. The Canyon is a mile in depth and the steep descending track often no more than three feet wide. There are cliff-walls and spurs where the rock-face gleams as with gold. "Fool's gold", the cowboy guide explains. "It's just mica ..."

As a sidelong route to Mexico, moreover, the Canyon had advantages, for the two coach travellers thus avoided the preposterous touristic carnival of Tijuana and the heavily Americanized Pacific highway, and an early morning start from Albuquerque swept them through the deserts of New Mexico to the frontier city which Americans call El Paso and the Mexicans style Ciudad Juarez. With

stamina, one could in fact coach south to Mexico City within twenty-
six hours, but the two young women preferred the more leisurely
stopover schedules, by the asphalt roads and the mountains, into the
Mexico where it hardly seems to matter whether one caught the first
coach or the next. This was the exotic traditional Mexico of thatched
houses and two-wheeled ox-carts, and the overnight stops brought
surprises, too, with industrial cities such as Monterrey and the surprising beauty, unexpected despite the tourist brochures, of such Spanish
colonial cities as San Luis Potosi. But the grand climax was, of course,
Mexico City itself, from which Princess Alexandra had written so
radiantly, with its brilliant light, its flowers and the fountains, glass
skyscrapers and gilded churches, the fantasy of the University buildings and the heady exhilaration of a city 7,000 feet high.

Katharine and Fiona zealously followed in Alexandra's footsteps,
visiting all the high spots the Princess praised. It was no hardship if the
day excursion to see the floating gardens of Xochimilco could be
covered only by sightseeing bus instead of royal limousine and, on the
Princess's recommendation, the girls drove another day through the
parrot-infested orchards to the immense ruins of Teotihuacan, with its
pyramids comparable to Egypt and vast esplanades of vanished
temples. Clambering across the huge sun-drenched stones, Katharine
knew that she was at a turning point of her life. For she would travel
no farther, but only homeward, back into the United States and the
Greyhound circuit again, by way of Laredo and San Antonio, in
Texas, by New Orleans to Charleston and Washington, D.C., and so
on the final stage of her journey home.

Alabama, Georgia, Carolina and Virginia, all were crossed in that
journey, the classic mansions and less classic hovels, the endless fields
and repetitive garish road stands, all were passed, every circuit of the
spinning wheels, every coach stop, every snack counter, taking her
closer now mile by mile to Edward. There is a story that before
leaving her hotel in Mexico City, she received one of the largest and
most beautiful bouquets of exotic flowers she had ever seen, with no
clue to the identity of the sender except the one initial "E" and
possibly Princess Alexandra with her brother and Fiona joined in a
romantic conspiracy to ensure that the flowers arrived in the right
place at the right time. On the way home, Katharine was also

welcomed by friends in Bermuda where, swimming and sun-bathing, she was able to soak the rush of travel out of her bones, while the surge and backwash of the surf dreamily obliterated the sustained and continuous turmoil of the road.

V

In Katharine's absence, the Duke of Kent was conspicuously attached more to cars than to girl friends and more to his soldiering career than to any diversions that many young bachelors might find in their spare time. The press, especially the columnists with their unceasing interest in royal romance, must have found it profitless to watch his activities when home on leave. He now had a bright red Jaguar, XK150, which was sufficiently conspicuous: he appeared at Zandvoort for the Dutch Grand Prix; he was seen on a test track at Stuttgart and at Silverstone and, as we know, he went to Goodwood car racing with his sister.

The two young people, however, had clearly demonstrated to their families that they were surviving the hazards of being apart. In May, Princess Marina had official occasion to visit Yorkshire to open a school and privately spent Whitsun not fifteen miles from Hovingham with her friends, Lord and Lady Feversham, at Nawton Tower. This opportunity saw an extremely happy meeting with the Worsleys and a calm review, as among elders, of the situation between the two young ones after six months of separation. "The young people have behaved perfectly," wrote a family friend, "it seems a shame to keep them apart for a moment longer than necessary, and yet we all feel it is for the best." Princess Marina's friends, indeed, began waiting, with some concern, for more definite news. The Duke of Kent celebrated his twenty-fourth birthday in Germany while on manoeuvres with the Royal Scots Greys. Princess Alexandra, having just concluded a highly successful goodwill tour in Australia and south-east Asia, flew home in time for his birthday convinced that it would be a day of reunion with Kate. But Edward was never one to shift regimental rotas and it was November before he returned home on two weeks' leave and his mother invited Katharine to dinner at Kensington Palace.

Princess Marina of course did not elect to become known as Princess

Marina, Duchess of Kent, until nearer the time of her son's marriage, but it becomes convenient to refer to her by her lifelong name. One doubts whether the change of title had yet crossed her mind; all that mattered was the happiness of the young people on their meeting, a happiness that "shone like a splendour", as one friend poetically said. Between mother and son there no longer lay the smallest shadow of difference nor of opposing view. However much Princess Marina had once pictured a future continental alliance for each of her children, she had invariably come to accept that in matters of the heart they would all three ultimately find their own way. It was a view she sympathetically took up without reluctance: had she not herself said, long ago, that she would never marry anyone except for love? Her one remaining doubt was that Eddie was still too young and fundamentally too inexperienced. "How the years pass . . . it seems only the other day he was a little boy," she was to write to an Athens friend.

This maternal sense of his youthfulness no doubt made her hope above all that he would still agree to wait a little longer and, a month or two before he returned from Hanover, an unexpected event gave her wishes both substance and sense. Edward, as I understand, wrote from Germany that he had not "changed his mind about K" and, in expressing her pleasure, his mother had added that there might yet be need for a little further patience, to be explained when they met.

The young man perhaps endured an agony of disquiet lest Katharine had changed her mind: some such conclusions can be drawn from the face of family circumstances. The elder generation were, in fact, suffering from a glut of young love that autumn. Princess Alexandra had obviously fallen in love with Angus Ogilvy, although the satisfactory outcome of that attachment still lay three years in the future. Even Fiona Myddelton was to be "deeply smitten" with Captain Alastair Aird, the Queen Mother's equerry, whom she married four years later. But the more immediate event was the private betrothal of Princess Margaret and Antony Armstrong-Jones. As I had cause to explain in my biography of Lord Snowdon,* this first stage of private betrothal may be better defined as an understanding, for the two had agreed to follow the traditional prudent system of the Royal Family and delay six months before a formal engagement. So relieved were

* *Lord Snowdon* (W. H. Allen), 1968.

the Duke of Kent and his Katharine to learn that nothing worse was to befall their own plans than waiting in line in a royal queue to the altar that this minor impediment only heightened their happiness.

Their own "understanding" remained in suspense, while they seemed to float on a cloud, content in the simple felicity of merely being together. Kate was staying with friends, perhaps with her Uncle Felix and Aunt Elizabeth at Henley, and Edward came over every morning in an inconspicuous Hillman "to go for a spin". "I expect you want to talk everything out," the Queen Mother said, when they went to Royal Lodge one day for lunch. There was so much to talk about, so much to tell. In Canada, Katharine had often imagined how it would be when the long separation came to an end. But in tangible reality events assumed an enchantment beyond imagining, wrapping them both in a gold foil of glamour.

The Queen Mother gave a dance at Clarence House, for instance, which would have seemed a dream to the Cinderella Kate who had worked at St Stephen's or to the schoolgirl of Runton Hill. The footmen wore the scarlet coats of semi-State livery; the dining-room became a glittering buffet, and a champagne bar was set up beneath the Strathmore portraits in the long corridor. A member of the household noted how the house "filled with the noise of clinking glasses, music and laughter . . . the popping champagne corks sounding like a shooting gallery . . ." Beneath the glittering chandeliers of the drawing-room on the first floor, more than a hundred couples danced to Ray Ellington's band.

The dance was given for no obvious reason, although it was really being held as one of the Queen Mother's happy gestures for Princess Margaret and today's Lord Snowdon, but the Duke of Kent and Katharine could indulge in the pretence that it was really their own party, their own homecoming reunion celebration, and the Queen and the Queen Mother sipped champagne with them, wishing them well, like fellow conspirators. The dancing went on until 3 a.m. and bacon and egg breakfasts were served to the happy untiring younger guests until nearly dawn. The following week, moreover, only forty-eight hours before Edward was due to return to Germany, the Queen gave a dinner and dance at Buckingham Palace, ostensibly to welcome Princess Alexandra home from Australia, but again in reality for

Princess Margaret and equally, in their own extra dimension of romance, for Eddie and Katharine.

I had occasion to note the presence of "Katharine Worsley, bright with the certitude of future happiness" and "scores of friends and kinsfolk, among them the Hamiltons and Herberts and Nevills and Toerrings and Beresfords. There was the young Marquess of Hamilton and Lord O'Neil, David Bailey and Angus and James Ogilvy. It was a wonderfully happy evening."

Lover's partings are such sweet sorrow, but Edward could say "I'll be back again in fourteen days". The time could be measured in glowing hours. On December 9th, he was given special leave of absence for his introduction as a peer to the House of Lords, his symbol of investiture as a royal duke into public service. Attended by Mr Philip Hay, he took the oath and subscribed the test roll before shaking hands with the Lord Chancellor and taking his seat, while his mother and sister, his younger brother and future wife watched from a gallery. The Queen Mother was a guest at the family party at Kensington Palace afterwards, when the big dining-room was cleared of all the books and maps and committee papers that usually littered the table and a happy group of twenty sat down to dinner.

"We must do everything for Miss Worsley to get to know us," the Queen Mother—Queen Elizabeth as she is always correctly known within the Royal Households—had observed to one of her ladies, and Katharine indeed had four royal sponsors, with Princess Marina, Princess Alexandra and the Princess Royal. Marina above all, now missed no opportunity to instruct her future daughter-in-law in all the intricacies of royal etiquette and protocol. There was the occasion, for instance, when the Lord Mayor of London gave a luncheon to Princess Alexandra at the Guildhall. The guests of honour included the Princess, Prince Philip and the Duke and Duchess of Gloucester, and among the less observed guests there were, I believe, Sir William and Lady Worsley, Sir Felix and Lady Brunner—and Katharine. Before this took place, the Kents were also at Sandringham for Christmas, and this saw the occasion when the Duke of Kent sought the Queen's permission to leave on the 28th and, as one of his intimates said, he "raced like a wild thing" to Hovingham Hall. He had not seen that beloved place nor visited Aunt Joyce at Cawton for nearly two years.

For a few days they were able to walk over the old paths and drive over the old familiar roads, spending hours of happiness too, at Cawton Hall itself, where Eddie never seemed to mind being disturbed by the children and every room seemed always littered by toys. And then the time came for another parting, and Katharine clearly understood that this was as it would always be, for an army officer's wife.

She celebrated her twenty-seventh birthday at home at Hovingham, in contrast to her working birthday in Toronto the previous year. Eddie was entering the Army ski championships with the Royal Scots Greys in Austria, where he won fourth place in both the slalom and downhill events and he 'phoned excitedly from the Tyrol with the birthday news that the engagement would be announced that week. He meant of course the official engagement of Princess Margaret and Antony Armstrong-Jones; a trimming of magic that it should come in the week of Katharine's own anniversary.

She was a guest at the wedding in Westminster Abbey on May 6th and with Eddie at the reception at Buckingham Palace afterwards: the nuptial festivities all around them, the speeches and toasts and laughter, again seemed an extra-dimensional scene to their own private happiness. Watching the superb pageantry of the scene in the Abbey, she must have tenderly pictured how Edward would take her hand at her own wedding and yet she still saw her own future in terms of such modest simplicity that she visualized a simple country ceremony in the far more homely setting of Hovingham church.

8 Edward and Katharine

Let sounds of Joy,
The Bridegroom's pain remove
The intruding hours employ,
With songs of Happy love.
The long, long wished for Day
Has crowned us with delight . . .

White, *Lyric to Handel's March in Scipio*
(The April chimes)

I

For the Duke of Kent the year 1960 was like a play in three acts, set against the regimental backgrounds of Germany and against the family scenes of Coppins and Hovingham, a three-act romantic comedy perhaps a little drawn out by the dramatist. The Duke could scarcely wait for the term of service in Germany to end. Promoted to temporary captain, he flew back to Dusseldorf three days after Princess Margaret's wedding, and in October, he assumed a role of State responsibility as an aide to the Queen for the State visit of King Mahendra of Nepal and his Queen. From a distance, intently studying the newspapers, Katharine watched the Duke going through the ceremonies of the reception at Gatwick Airport, the State Banquet, the gala opera at Covent Garden, the tours of Army inspection. Princess Alexandra in that same month represented the Queen at the independence ceremonies of the new Federation of Nigeria. Many factors had influenced the Queen's advisers in proposing the Kents for these duties, but no better opportunity could have been found had they wished to point a cautionary tale of the tasks that a new Duchess of Kent might anticipate during her working life.

The Duke flew back to Germany on October 23rd, though not before telling Katharine that he would also have to be away in May to attend the independence ceremonies in Sierra Leone. "In May?"

she must have questioned, not without disquiet and concern. For there had been so much left unspoken and taken for granted, and it had seemed that the month of May—just a year after Princess Margaret's wedding—would see her own marriage. The date had however been suggested and fixed in distant Sierra Leone. Such was the subjection of royalty to rule and custom, to protocol and the world-wide processes of constitutional law.

Happily, the picture had a brighter side. The Royal Scots Greys were shortly returning from Germany at last, and the Duke was to be posted to the War Office early in the new year. This implied everything for, apart from the Sierra Leone arrangements, he would be home, if not for good, at least into the foreseeable future. This approaching milestone released a torrent of excitement and jubilation. Katharine had seemed to spend all her time writing to Germany or hurrying across to the Hovingham post-office in the November rain to enquire for letters before the postman could bring them. And then on November 25th, Eddie unexpectedly telephoned from London airport, highly delighted because he had arrived forty-eight hours earlier than was thought. Should he come up to Yorkshire—or would she come to London? Such was the tenor of their conversation. Kate had been planning to come to London and would catch an earlier train. "It was like all their meetings," says a friend, "they could never contain their excitement, never waste a minute..."

Katharine reached Kensington Palace and paid off the taxi. She gaily acknowledged the salute of the usual friendly policeman. The steward opened the door: "His Royal Highness is expecting you!" She heard the sound of Edward's footsteps and then a crash and a yell of pain. He had fallen on the stairs in his rush to her side and, she had to help him to his feet while, laughing and rueful, he clung to her, grimacing with mingled pleasure and pain.

As the doctors discovered when they arrived, he had broken a bone in his foot. Alexandra and Katharine spent the weekend teasing him about it, while the wretched victim sat with his foot in plaster supported on a stool. "I'm always tumbling about," said Princess Marina, "and now Eddie, too!" It was such an absurd and preposterous climax to his long-awaited "homecoming for good". Except that in Edward's life, no homecoming ever seemed permanent after all.

He was concerned about the army ski championships again in January, while his womenfolk taunted him with solemn forecasts that he would have to ski on crutches. He safely recovered nevertheless and, with all the Kent family, was at the Queen's house-party at Sandringham for Christmas. The *Court Circular* subsequently appeared with the unusual footnote that fifteen of the Royal Family celebrated Christmas together and, occurring on a Sunday, Christmas Day—Princess Alexandra's birthday—was also made the unusual occasion of a ceremonial when, to quote the *Circular* the Queen "conferred upon the Duke of Kent the dignity of a Knight Grand Cross of the Royal Victorian Order and invested his Royal Highness with the Insignia of the Order . . . Her Majesty also conferred upon Princess Alexandra of Kent the dignity of a Dame Grand Cross of the Royal Victorian Order and invested her Royal Highness with the Insignia of the Order". What the *Circular* did not mention was that the Duke of Kent also had something further to ask the Queen, namely, her formal consent to his marriage. Under the Royal Marriages Act he had been required to seek the Queen's consent until attaining the age of twenty-five, and he was in fact now twenty-five and two months, but the courtesy was still to be observed.

It was customary for the Kents to leave Sandringham soon after Christmas to see the New Year in at Coppins in the old Russian style, but the Duke once again left earlier than usual—indeed, on Boxing Day itself—to drive, in a grey Jaguar now, to Hovingham. The family at the Hall detected the suppressed excitement in his manner. On New Year's Day, he and Katharine went out as usual, the dogs at their heels, apparently with the intention of walking to Aunt Joyce's and no one suspected that they had returned to the house and to the quiet of the library. The family often gathered there for drinks before lunch and the grandfather clock on the stairs had chimed mid-day with its first chiming tune of the year, "When I survey Clarinda's charms, Folded within my circling arms . . ."* The story is that Katharine's parents went into the room and found Eddie and Kate perched like children on the single-seater stool before the

* "Love Triumphant", an alternative lyric to a Minuet by Handel.

fire, both looking full of mischief, and then Lady Worsley saw the ring brilliantly twinkling upon her daughter's hand, a superb sapphire upon platinum, flanked by the flashing white fire of large single diamonds.

After the congratulations, the joyful good wishes, they 'phoned Aunt Joyce and her husband to come over from Cawton "just to hear some news". Oliver was due for lunch, and Marcus and his wife drove over from Wool Knoll. The cook had not expected so many to lunch and I am told there was hardly enough to go round at that happy, impromptu party—and of course the betrothal still had to remain a family secret for a month or two more. The illusion of "everything as usual" was successfully maintained when the Duke left with the Scots Greys ski team for Austria a few days later.

Princess Marina and Princess Alexandra were to be seen at St Moritz for the culminating ski championships, with no sign of Kate. In London, indeed, she indulged in a festive round of theatre and dinner parties with family and friends, and her parents presently looked around for a small house in Kensington which they could rent as a suitable town base in readiness for coming events.

In mufti, a member of the bowler-hat brigade, the Duke took up his staff job at the War Office on February 13th, the first member of the Royal Family to work there since the Duke of Cambridge ceased to be Commander-in-Chief in 1895, as commentators were quick to point out. The Duke of Kent, they said, "wore cars" as other people wore uniforms, and he turned up on the first day in a suitably conventional Austin Seven, a model judiciously "hotted up" however beneath the white bonnet. A week later, Marcus and Bridget Worsley celebrated Katharine's twenty-eighth birthday with a dinner-party at their home in Flood Street, Chelsea, with none to watch the comings-and-goings of their guests. Marcus was then Parliamentary Private Secretary to the Minister of Health, lunching a private guest once or twice a week at the Carlton Club. Oliver and Eddie were equally unobtrusive when they lunched together at the Cavalry Club. The Duke was more conspicuous that week when he attended an Army Estimates debate in the House, an engagement in the line of duty. And then on the evening of March 8th, 1961, the Court Circular included an announcement from Kensington Palace, "It is with the greatest pleasure that the Duchess of Kent announces the betrothal of her elder son, Prince Edward, Duke of Kent, to Katharine, only daughter of Sir William and Lady Worsley, to which union the Queen has gladly given her consent."

II

"We are all very happy about it as he has loved Katharine for four years," Princess Marina wrote to a friend. "It is a good beginning, I feel, and she is a pretty, sweet person, so I thank God for another great blessing."

The response of the public to Katharine precisely matched these sentiments. A royal engagement is launched only after dire delays, as we have seen, but there is no deliberate attempt to put over the new product, no skilfully staged introduction, no insidious attempt by any royal secretariat to mould public opinion, yet Katharine was given an unmistakable welcome. The phenomenon was perhaps all the stranger in that she was totally unknown to "the world and his wife", seldom noticed in the social columns, with no long press record in the libraries of Fleet Street. The public learned only that she was a Yorkshire girl, "the squire's daughter", a sensible, good-natured girl, blonde and extremely pretty, and yet the photographs also showed that her looks had a touch of originality. The only impulse to public favour was that the press and TV cameras at Kensington Palace also lingered on Princess Marina and Princess Alexandra, and some of their popularity immediately glistened upon the newcomer. But the engagement drew, too, upon older residual links of affection, stemming back twenty years to the handsome and tragic figure of the Duke of Kent's father.

There was also the factor that, after a phase of apparent youthful irresponsibility, the young Duke had settled down, showing himself both disciplined and dutiful, royal qualities always held in respect by British public opinion. The trimmings around the young couple all added up in the sum total of romantic regard: the choice of the sapphire engagement ring, the symbol of true love; the hint of difficulties faced and overcome. The television cameras brought

Katharine an instant national debut. But it also appeared auspicious, as I mentioned in a national Sunday newspaper series at the time, that "within a week of the avowed betrothal the Duke of Kent and his fiancée officially appeared together at the state dinner at Buckingham Palace for the Commonwealth Premiers. One by one the representative leaders of all the Commonwealth peoples congratulated the happy pair and wished them well."

The public welcomed the thought of the new recruit, the young commoner, supposedly unaccustomed to royal glamour, being thrown in at the deep end, and it was in fact Katharine's first experience of Court formality. Eleven separate tables had been arranged in the white and gold Palace ballroom, with a member of the Royal Family at each. Dr Verwoerd had just sadly announced South Africa's withdrawal from the Commonwealth; and Sir Michael Adeane, the Queen's secretary, valued the brightening of the atmosphere which the congenial presence of the young engaged couple brought to the reception. At the State dinner, attentive to an African gentleman on her right, Katharine was irresistibly reminded, I think, of a Christmas dinner at St Stephen's orphanage.

The early announcement that the wedding would take place in York Minster on June 8th similarly found high favour with the public. The press was quick to discover that no royal wedding had been held in York Minster for 633 years, not indeed since Edward III was married to Philippa, daughter of the Count of Hainault, in 1328, and the precedent entailed a happy coincidence, for a son of that marriage was to gain warrior fame as the Black Prince and his bride in 1361 was, oddly enough, a Countess of Kent. This frail link was recounted over and over while, by a fine irony, the Romeo and Juliet touch that charmed the family was barely mentioned. A descendant of Charles the First was marrying a descendant of Oliver Cromwell. From ancient grudge, a pair of starry-eyed lovers indeed revised the fatal story of the Montagues and Capulets. Both families imagined that the romantic and charming comparison would gain wide attention, yet few pens made the point save mine.

A more prosaic comment on York's shortage of royal weddings was equally not readily obvious to the laity. Some members of the Worsley family had been baptized in the Minster but in recent times none had been married there, for York Minster was not in fact licensed for weddings at all.

This presented a poser. Katharine, we know had visualized a simple ceremony in All Saints, Hovingham, but the church would scarcely seat two hundred people. The Queen made it known at an early stage that she would be happy to come to Yorkshire, a marriage in the Minster seemed ideal on every count, and the ecclesiastical difficulty could be smoothly overcome. Application had only to be made to the Faculty Office for a special license, available upon the approval of the Archbishop of Canterbury for a marriage "at any place at any time". The date of the wedding, however, created a dilemma with a more definite cliff-hanging quality, for the Archbishop of Canterbury, Dr Fisher, was retiring on May 31st and the Archbishop of York, Dr Ramsey, then became Archbishop-Designate of Canterbury, although he would not be enthroned until June 27th. One private suggestion was for May 8th, 301 years to the day since the proclamation of Charles II, but this was a Monday, with its obvious difficulties and conflicted with the Queen's State Visit to Italy. June 8th was eventually agreed as an ideal date.

Is there ever a wedding without problems? Sir William and Lady Worsley agreed that the white roses of York were indispensable for the decoration of the Minster, but no grower in Yorkshire could guarantee to provide the thousand white half-open buds which the florists estimated would be required. Ultimately white and palest yellow blooms were grown under glass at the Blaby Rose Gardens in Leicestershire. Then there was the added difficulty that much of the Minster was wrapped in scaffolding during the vast task of post-war repairs and renewals—but Dean Milner-White promised that the church could be sufficiently in order by the day.

Fortunately, the young couple were not too deeply involved in these problems. Katharine was to become dreamily absorbed in the details of her wedding-gown, the shining outward material of which, a silk gauze woven with irridescent thread, was chosen well ahead of time and specially woven for her in France. It suffices that Katharine and Edward were free now incautiously to enjoy the pleasures of their engagement. They were espied one night sitting inconspicuously in a box at the ballet at Covent Garden and, after the final curtain, the entire audience turned to applaud them The Queen and the Duke of Edinburgh gave an exceptional house-party at Windsor Castle with the then King and Queen of the Hellenes and their daughters, the Princesses Sophia and Irene, and the Kent family and Katharine as their principal dinner guests, and "Kate at the Castle" seemed a Heaven-sent headline to newspaper editors.

The public little realized that, within a few days, the Duke of Kent's visit to Sierra Leone to represent the Queen in the independence celebrations, abruptly reduced Kate to desperate subjection to television and newspapers for word of him. It was as if recent events had all been a dream and she were still back in Toronto. His nightly telephone call seemed always to occur in the midst of an intensive electric storm, and his week's absence seemed harder to bear than months apart. Yet his mission was a notable success. The Lord Mayor and City Corporation of London gave a lunch at the Mansion House to mark his return and Katharine found herself once more on the dream-like plane of so many of her engagement events.

The gilded invitation card appeared to invite Miss Katharine Worsley alone but Edward warned her with mock severity not to count on it. And when she arrived with him at the Mansion House, the pavements were packed with people; the Lord Mayor and his Lady Mayoress (Sir Bernard and Lady Waley-Cohen) and the Sheriffs were waiting in welcome and Kate found herself, as if in a dream indeed, waving from the portico balcony to acknowledge the crowds. Then more remarkable, as they made their way to the Egyptian Room, they were greeted with loud hand-clapping by aldermen and guests, robed judges beaming and applauding, gowned officials breaking into smiles, all intended formality quite forgotten.

It was characteristic that soon after Katharine returned home to the Kensington mews house which her father had rented, there was a telephone call from her sister-in-law, Bridget, begging her not to come to Wool Knoll over the weekend because two-year-old Sarah had mumps. Intermeshed with what Edward called "full dress", the sweeter family events went on. In the autumn of their first meeting, Katharine and Edward had gone to the coming-out dance of June

Shepherd-Cross and now they went together to her wedding in Hovingham Church. During Kate's absence in Canada, Eddie had attended the wedding of a West Country friend and now they went there for the weekend to admire the new baby.

By way of another domestic event, in the midst of the wedding preparations, Aunt Joyce also had a baby boy and, only five days before the wedding, the Duke of Kent was godfather to the nine-weeks-old Giles Worsley at the Hovingham font. Of all Aunt Joyce's elder children, it seemed appropriate that Katharine's god-daughter, seven-year-old Diana, should be her bridesmaid. Another god-daughter bridesmaid was four-year-old Emily Briggs, neé Colegate. Then there was Sandra Butter, the daughter of those good Perthshire friends who had patiently counselled Edward and Katharine at a critical juncture. From her bridegroom's side, Katharine asked Princess Anne to be chief bridesmaid, with Joanna Fitzroy, Jane Spencer and Katherine Ashley Cooper. (The three pages were Simon Hay, Edward Beckett and Marcus's son, William.) And from Toronto there came six-year-old Willa, so much a Worsley in looks and character and, at the airport, very nearly knocking her aunt off her feet with the boisterous affection of her greeting.

The half-hour at Heathrow spent waiting for John and his family to arrive indeed betokened all the difficulties of Katharine's new situation. Parking her car, she had checked the incoming flights and sat on a settee in the arrivals hall, patiently waiting, as she had often waited for John and Carolyn at other times. But now she became aware of the people dawdling as they walked around her, surveying her, the growing buzz of interest, and then the ever-present camera-man circling to get a clear view for a photoflash. "It will not do", Lady Worsley would have said, in such a situation. Katharine judged it best to get up and stroll over to the departure desk, and was instantly recognized. "I don't want any fuss," she said quietly. An official opened a door marked "Staff only" and said, "Perhaps, ma'am, you would prefer to wait in the Queen's Building?" She accepted but went impetuously onto the tarmac to greet them on being told that Mr and Mrs Worsley were being brought to her. "What's all this?" said John, as he saw the glint of tears in her eyes.

It was not only happiness at seeing him again. It was that, already, as Edward had foretold, she had to be protected a little from the affection and curiosity that surrounds and hedges all the Royal Family.

II

It was snowing on the day Katharine Worsley was born and it rained on her wedding morning. "Only showers, you'll see," her father reassured her; and her brother, Oliver, coming up just after breakfast, was content to say in his quiet, firm way that everything was in order. Even Willa, who had been put to bed with a temperature the day before, was feeling better. The public took it for granted that a royal wedding should run smoothly; people imagined an array of hard-working personnel behind the scenes. The firmer reality was that everything at Hovingham was organized by Oliver Worsley, and the family was amused that a bachelor should stage-manage a wedding so well. He had, of course, the unstinted help and advice of Sir Philip Hay, Princess Marina's secretary, who was in turn in liaison with the Lord Chamberlain's office and Buckingham Palace, and Sir William Worsley personally kept in touch with the civic officials in York and the authorities of York Minster. But it was Oliver who took a load of responsibility from his father's shoulders—Sir William was then seventy-one—and light-heartedly pretended that after handling Katharine's musical festivals her marriage was merely child's play.

It helped to be able to commandeer the Worsley Arms but in fact the hotel has only twelve bedrooms, and Cawton Hall and Wool Knoll were never more crowded. Every large country home for miles around had its contingent of guests, and rooms were sought from Helmsley to Malton by reporters, photographers, caterers and others with wedding business. The bridegroom, with his mother, his sister and his brother, who was to be best man, stayed with the Earl and Countess of Feversham at Nawton Hall. The Queen and Prince Philip and most of the other royal guests were to arrive at York by special train. One group had even chartered a helicopter, and the mere deployment of hundreds of cars upon the Minster at a given hour meant rigid control of traffic routes by police and auxiliaries over a twenty miles radius.

Though not always directly concerned, Oliver Worsley was astonished at the wide range and intricacy of the difficulties involved. The fanfare of trumpeters and the guard of honour of the Royal Scots Greys entailed an Army convoy from Catterick. The York conservative club hospitably offered a sanctum for bridesmaids and nannies while, at a more personal point of the planning spectrum, the designer of the soft and voluminous wedding veil, Mr Reed Crawford, overlooked no contingency and made three bridal veils, one for rehearsals, one for the ceremony and a reserve for emergencies or in case the bride needed a crisp fresh veil for Cecil Beaton's photographic session at Hovingham Hall.

It was being said that Katharine Worsley was a strong-willed personality, a girl with a mind of her own, but this was a counterpart of the fiction that the Duke of Kent was the weaker character. Indeed, Kate was greatly distressed that nearly every newspaper announced in large headlines that she would not promise to "obey" her husband. The misunderstanding came about because the modern version of the marriage service was to be used, although bride and groom had in reality asked for the vow of obedience to be included. There was more substance to the story of the young couple's careful choice of music. It seemed such a good idea at first to include a setting of the 45th Psalm by a Yorkshire composer, until Katharine discovered with dismay the phrase "Forget also thine own people and thy father's house", and evidently the anthem was omitted.

For her wedding-dress, Katharine had unhesitatingly sought Princess Marina's counsel and on her advice the gown was commissioned from John Cavanagh, who also designed both Marina's and Princess Alexandra's dresses and coats for the occasion. Cavanagh when very young had commenced his career with Molyneux in Paris and first met Princess Marina when Molyneux was designing her wedding gown. Trained in this classic tradition, he subsequently became chief designer to Pierre Balmain and then gained Princess Marina's prompt and encouraging patronage when he set up his own house in London in 1952. Katharine's gown, said Mr Cavanagh was "an essay in bridal simplicity with the formality and importance required by a royal occasion in a magnificent setting". The gossamer and shimmering white silk French gauze was mounted within layers of organdie, and the opalescent theme flowed into a double train fifteen feet in length. The effect was enchanting; Katharine had never looked more beautiful. And, as a commentator reported from the Minster, "a friendly chuckle ran through the congregation at the bridegroom's expression of delight when she made her entry".

But that delight was reflected in every village, at every cottage gate, as Katharine and her father rode by on their way from Hovingham Hall to York Minster. Katharine wore the single strand of perfect pearls that her parents had given her, and the diadem, once Queen Mary's, that was the wedding gift of Princess Marina. The rain ceased and the sun shone, save for a final indignant flurry of hailstones flung at the church doors while the ceremony proceeded. And the bridegroom? In the scarlet and blue ceremonial uniform of the Royal Scots Greys, he looked every inch a royal duke in splendour and had never seemed so handsome.

To one of the senior royal guests, Queen Victoria's grand-daughter, Queen Eugenie of Spain, "Young Katharine was simply adorable, glittering and very blonde." To the distinguished historian, Roger Fulford, the bride and her father "gave an impression of touching devotion" in their long walk up the aisle. John Cavanagh knew that the bride had lost four pounds in weight in the anxiety of preparation and knew from her smile after the ceremony that all strain had vanished. To cheers and the skirl of bagpipes the couple drove away, to be followed by three Queens and more Crown Princes, princes and princesses, royal dukes and duchesses than any commentator could count.

At Hovingham Hall the wedding reception was staged like a garden party on those ancient lawns; and with the great marquees, the umbrella-topped tables and the two thousand guests strolling about, champagne glasses in hand, it eclipsed any scene ever staged in the garden of Buckingham Palace. As one of the bridesmaids triumphantly discovered, even the china pigs seemed to be enjoying themselves, gazing down from the nursery window.

In the early evening the married couple left by car—with their two dogs, Charles and Columbus—for the R.A.F. airfield at Linton where a Heron of the Queen's Flight was waiting to fly them on the first stage of their honeymoon. "A pleasant flight, your Royal Highness," murmured one of the airfield officers, in bidding Katharine farewell. For an instant she had imagined that he was talking to her husband and then realized he was addressing her. Until that moment, despite family playfulness, I believe she was hardly aware that she was now the Duchess of Kent. In the happiness of the day, in the emotion and the excitement, she had not given a thought to the strange translation that she was Katharine Worsley no longer.

IV

"Would you . . . perhaps . . . care to spend . . . the first part of your honeymoon . . . at Birkhall?" the Queen Mother had asked, in her charming way. The Duke of Kent could have thought of nothing better. Birkhall was linked with the happy summers of his boyhood just after the war, when the King and Queen—his Uncle Bertie and Aunt Elizabeth—regarded it as their private Scottish home, where they enjoyed a secluded happiness that hardly seemed possible at Balmoral. They had always filled every room with closest family and friends and, while a new wing was being built, the young Duke of Kent retained the liveliest memories of being ensconced in a magnificent trailer parked in the grounds. The house was a tall, colour-washed Jacobite charmer, built on a hillside with wide-spreading views, a house full of log fireplaces yet furnished in a light, modern way. There were wonderful walks to the salmon-leap at the Falls of Muick and into the wilds of Glen Muick itself. To the informed, Balmoral Castle was but a screen, a protective cover, to the enchantment of Birkhall. All this the Duke had told his bride, and she was indeed to agree that "It was made for a honeymoon".

The present Queen had herself once called the old house "the nicest place in the whole world", in writing to a friend, but first her bon voyage message of happiness greeted the newly-weds inside the royal aircraft with three bottles of champagne, ready on ice at her wish, and a pile of smoked salmon sandwiches. The honeymooners realized they were hungry and, with the help of the air crew, the bulk of these provisions were demolished on the 90-minute flight. To one member of the family it seemed characteristic Worsley weather when Katharine wrote from Birkhall that they had flown through a thunderstorm. At Dyce airport, a further surprise awaited the honeymooners, for they had not foreseen that hundreds of people would be waiting to cheer them or indeed that there would be people smiling and waving, flinging confetti and flowers, along all the fifty miles through Deeside.

The Queen and Prince Philip spent part of their honeymoon at Birkhall when the house was entrenched in deep early snow, and Princess Alexandra and Angus Ogilvy were similarly to honeymoon there two years later. The housekeeper, Annie Gordon, knew, and none better, how to follow a curtsey with a motherly welcome. What is it to us if the Duke and Duchess delayed supper and went to stroll in the garden in the gathering dusk? Their wedding-day had been a Thursday and it is said that they drove an estate-car into Ballater the following day to buy a birthday card for the Duke of Edinburgh, who was forty that Saturday. On Monday the honeymooners read that crowds waiting to see them at Crathie Church had been disappointed. Was there some slight hint of a sabbatarian frown? At all events, the newly-wed couple made a point of attending morning service at Crathie the following Sunday before they flew south to continue their honeymoon in Majorca.

Although it had been widely mooted that they would again travel in a plane of the Queen's Flight, the Duke preferred to stave off any possible criticism of public expenditure by arranging a private charter plane. This entailed a four-hour flight, the meagre official travel allowance was still in force, and both the Duke and his new Duchess were aware of their personal budget needs, but Mr Whitney Straight was benevolently lending them the Villa Quiros, itself the scene of as many romantic honeymoons as Birkhall. Prince Albert and Princess Paola of Belgium had commenced their wedded life there two years before, as had Sir Anthony Eden and his wife some years earlier. Comparatively remote from the touristic carnival of modern Majorca, the north-east peninsula of Formentor is still magically a world alone, with vistas of mountain, forests and craggy cliff around a transparent blue bay.

For three weeks, the Kents were free to revel in this paradise, to swim and sun-bathe, laze and relax. They swam alternately in the sea and the swimming-pool. They tried out the blue speedboats that awaited their pleasure at the jetty; they sometimes played evening tennis and browsed trough the Villa's library of records. They had the fun of lunching unrecognized on the terrace of the nearby luxe Hotel Formentor and of dancing there a few nights later. They rode and water-skied. They sun-bathed a little too much at first, so that the news travelled round the world that the Duchess of Kent had a mild attack of sunstroke. It was truly a royal honeymoon and yet, on July 7th, when they returned to Coppins, it was of course "wonderful to be home".

9 Wife and Mother

Cordelio, generous, prudent wife
The sprightly dame did thus advise:
Fidelio's sighs she must approve.
And when she Crowned his constant love,
Enchanting sounds dwelt on her Tongue,
Enchanting sounds, etc.

The White Joak, sung by Mrs
Roberts at the Theatre in Drury
Lane, the words by Mr Davis
(The June chimes)

I

It is a merit of Coppins that it lies only a few miles from London airport, yet sufficiently far from the flight paths, within a rural enclave of Buckinghamshire, to be a remove from aircraft noise. The sound is always there, like the wind in the trees or the muted hum of traffic on the motorway. But "one gets used to it" and "one is within fifteen minutes, plus flying time, of anywhere in the world", as the Kents like to say. The Duke and Duchess of Kent returned from their honeymoon early in July. Their plane touched down at 4.45 and shortly after five o'clock they turned into the Coppins drive to find the pleasant cream-washed, green-shuttered house flag-bedecked and en fête for their return, with a sign across the entrance-way to bid them "Welcome Home".

Coppins* was the house where the Duke's parents had commenced their married life, a bequest from their aunt, Princess Victoria, Queen Alexandra's spinster daughter. It had been built originally by John Mitchell, of the Ashton and Mitchell theatre ticket fame, a rambling multi-gabled Victorian house, which the Duke of Kent, Princess Marina's husband, had converted with taste and skill and, under his

* The fuller story of Coppins is told in *Princess Alexandra* by Helen Cathcart, 1967.

will, it became the present Duke's property on coming of age. Princess
Marina had continued to live there but she always said that she would
never be a resident mother-in-law and, to the family surprise, she
moved out quite unemotionally when the time came, even to selling
the bulk of her hobbyist collections—the Fabergé treasures, jewelled
cigarette cases, antique fans and Czarist silver—at auction at
Sotheby's.

Later, it was to be blithely calculated that the combined age of the
four female staff whom the very young butler had lined up to greet
the new chatelaine totalled 240 years. The two eldest had been present
at Prince Michael's christening at Windsor nearly nineteen years
before, an occasion when King George of Greece found himself
puzzled at not knowing anybody and was told, "No wonder—they
are the Coppins staff". To the new Duchess they were, however,
already old friends. The strangeness was to find Princess Marina
absent, the house no longer drenched in turkish cigarette smoke, and,
in the entrance hall, the sweet perfume of humea, the incense plant,
now gaining its own. The house had always been Edward's home, and
now it was Katharine's, her poodle Charles came running in and out
with Edward's Columbus, and her maid, Lilian, began taking the bags
for unpacking.

One or two local people came to welcome the newly-weds, and it is
remembered that the young couple that evening went first to the
music room where their wedding gifts had been assembled, and almost
immediately began carrying lamps and trinkets and china upstairs and
down. Katharine had wondered whether she could leave a bride's list
at Fortnum's and had been reassured by Princess Margaret, "Why
not? I did!" She had diffidently begun her list, "Two hand-painted
tooth-brush mugs, one monogrammed 'E' and the other 'K'; two
Foley breakfast-in-bed sets, pink Rutland pattern, with coffee pots;
Crown Staffordshire early morning set for two, dogwood pattern; a
large thermos jug; a pint thermos flask . . ." and now here was each
well-wishing token. The brandy glasses "but no decanter, please" and
the Spode Luneville jumbo cups and saucers, the ice bowl and the
table mats, the two silver napkin rings from the indoor staff at
Hovingham Hall, the six silver ashtrays and matchbox covers from
Hovingham village, the long low leather-topped table from the Royal

Household flanked by the wicker sedan garden chairs from Uncle Eddy and Aunt Joyce . . . A new blue car, an acceptable gift from Ford's, already stood in the garage. Princess Alexandra's gift, a double bed which unzipped into singles was already installed in the big main bedroom. And then there were, as one personal record noted, "the mountains of glass . . . silver ornaments and candlesticks, paintings, books, food trolleys, trays, kitchenware, saucepans and sheets . . ."

Invited for the weekend, on returning from Italy, Princess Marina was agreeably surprised at the change her daughter-in-law had brought to the house: an extra quality of light as in the old days, new space and ingenuity in the planning of the rooms, although so much was sweetly unchanged. The Princess's portrait still hung over the desk in the drawing-room, although the desk was different; her husband's portrait still commanded the opposite wall, near the grand piano, but a framed Worsley photograph stood on the marble-topped side-table. On the shelves the family collection of early English porcelain had been rearranged to rather better effect. The same delicate bird pictures still enhanced the hall but elsewhere there hung a set of military prints which had featured among the wedding gifts. Eddie had put them up, Katharine explained, "not too easy with me shaking the ladder."

Princess Marina may not have noticed every subtle new emphasis, for no change had been made merely for change' sake by the young couple. Agreed new redecoration had been undertaken in their absence and Marina admired the new guest-room schemes, some in pink and some in blue. The Duke used his father's old separate bedroom only as a dressing-room: "I can sleep alone when I'm in barracks." Probably on her first visit as an admiring mama-in-law Marina did not enter her husband's study. Had she done so, she would have found his desk undisturbed as always, the faded note in his handwriting still there, perhaps the last memo he ever wrote. "Please do not move anything on this desk." Nor did Princess Marina enter the kitchens, and when she did so, some months later, it was to find the greatest change of all.

The new Duchess of Kent was indeed dismayed on first seeing the service quarters, where it seemed that little could have changed since the portrait of Queen Victoria was first hung in the housekeeper's room. The cook managed with a gas stove of ancient pattern, the maids coped with stone-flagged floors and royal comptrollers had kept a zealous eye on domestic expenditure for decades. Even Eddie, it seems, was guilty of proposing that a television set of extreme vintage would still do for the staff sitting-room. The central heating in the staff wing was somewhat meagre, and the Duchess stipulated extra coal-fires in the bedrooms until electric convectors could be installed. Husband and wife had agreed they would prefer a butler younger than themselves and the Duke's former valet was promoted. This did not fully work out and a strained household was eventually put in order by a former houseman who had once worked at Coppins under Bysouth, Princess Marina's steward. Pleasantly, too, a deputation from Iver village welcomed the young couple home at a ceremony in the local sports field, and presented an address of welcome framed in red, white and blue and a three-volume work on water-fowl of the world. This gift was inspired perhaps by a small water-garden at Coppins fed from the local River Colne, and the roar of a passing plane evoked laughter in the Duchess's response when she said that she felt at home already.

II

It was claimed that the newly-weds led the life of an ordinary married couple at Coppins, but not every young couple can receive the Queen and Prince Philip to dinner on Saturday night or drive over to tea on Sunday with the Queen Mother. Every weekday morning, the Duke would leave the house sharp at 8.40 to drive to Whitehall in his white Austin, arriving at the War Office at 9.25. Every evening, unless a later conference detained him, he returned at 6.30 and would let himself into the house by the side door, calling "Porgy! Porgy darling!", while his orderly garaged the car.

The press early discovered that his new chauffeur was in fact a young corporal in the Royal Scots Greys, and to a critical enquirer the War Office press officer had to explain that it was a long-established custom for soldiers to be made available as orderlies to royal personages if they could be spared. Corporal Milne indeed became for a time one of the cheerful, indispensable personalities of Coppins, washing the cars or exercising the dogs in his spare hours, assisting, too, in the great bonfire when years of junk were carried down from the attics. On her day for hairdressing appointments with Rene, the Duchess usually drove into town with her husband, and was free for shopping and lunch with a friend. The freedom, one may add, was relative. Customers recognized her in shops and she shrank equally from the stares or the politely averted gaze. She fastidiously began to avoid main streets and had to don an entirely alien mantle of pretence, pretending not to notice the eyes that sharply swivelled in the lift at Harrods or the occasional "double take" of passers-by in Sloane Street. The mantle was to thicken like a second skin. Going home to Hovingham, ahead of the Duke, one weekend, she arranged innocently to meet her father at King's Cross and arrived to find him involved with a young man, clearly a reporter, who was asking questions. "It gives me a shrinking, sinking feeling," she told a friend.

The Women's Institute at Iver lost no time in inviting her to membership and her then secretary—in reality, Princess Marina's assistant secretary, Lieut. N. J. S. Hunt—wrote in reply that she was not taking up public engagements "for the time being". This caused a tiny ripple in the Iver dovecotes. "They are calling you the reluctant Duchess," a friend reported. Whereupon the Duchess promptly telephoned the branch president to say that she would take great pleasure in joining the branch and, yes, would be happy to come to a meeting to see a demonstration of cooking "savoury snacks". It would have been like any similar engagement at Hovingham, except that royalty must arrive neither too late nor too soon, and for this first small essay in duty, the Duchess caused a flurry by unexpectedly arriving ten minutes early.

Her husband had to laugh her out of worrying about the resulting newspaper headlines. More pleasantly, a Cheshire nurseryman asked permission to name a new rose "Katharine Worsley" and a bouquet of the clustered red blooms arrived shortly after the return home from Majorca. There were pleasures as well as penalties in royal prestige. A hundred white and cream rose bushes of the variety used in York Minster came from Blaby and the planting of the new rose border became an early autumn preoccupation.

The Duke of Kent's own reaction to married life was one of heightened responsibility expressed—as Thomas Worsley might have done—through his own youthful enthusiasms. He had safety belts

fitted to the front seats of his cars and, on taking delivery of a new
E-type Jaguar, he passed the advanced driving test of the Institute of
Advanced Motorists. Katharine characteristically spent many an afternoon in the garden, weeding, in a pair of old slacks, and eager on his
return to take him to see her efforts. One may trace in the Duke at this
time the psychological quirk that everything at Coppins should be so
far as possible as it was in his father's day, as he remembered it from
earliest boyhood. Ridout, the gardener, agreed that there had once been
a rose-bed under the dining-room window and so roses were replaced
there. For economy's sake two greenhouses had been added to the
original one to provide extra produce, but the Duke had the additions
knocked down. Far across the lawn, a little summerhouse of classical
Georgian pattern had undergone damage from horses and cattle and
fallen into disuse, but the Duke set his heart on having it repaired and
repainted in time for his twenty-six birthday, and tea was served there
on the eve of his anniversary, a Sunday. Katharine, too, put into action
precepts she had learned from her mother. The Hovingham staff, for
instance, enjoyed the freedom of the grounds, except the family rose
garden, and the Duchess similarly reserved a Coppins rose arbour when
she wished to enjoy family privacy.

Probably Katharine's greatest domestic responsibility that autumn
was a lively family dinner-party to mark Princess Alexandra's departure
on a Far East tour which was to take her to Hong Kong, Tokio,
Bangkok, Rangoon, Aden and Tripoli. On her safe return, the Duke
and Duchess echoed the occasion with a dinner-party to celebrate
Princess Marina's fifty-fifth birthday, a doubly memorable family event
for, in proposing his mother's health, the Duke gaily mentioned
another mama and turned with twinkling eyes to Katharine. The
Queen and Lady Worsley and, inevitably, Aunt Joyce, were also told of
the happy anticipations that same weekend.

All the Kents went as usual to Sandringham for Christmas and on
Christmas Day—Princess Alexandra's birthday—they attended morning service at the parish church across the park. The Duchess had been
reluctant to give her hopes wider publicity but, during the service, she
felt unwell and had to leave, escorted by the young Prince of Wales.
Next day it was announced from Coppins that the Duchess of Kent was
expecting a child in the summer.

II

The Duke of Kent was to captain the Royal Scots Greys ski team at St Moritz in January, 1962, and his wife startled some of the family by saying she would be going with him. The hotel rooms were booked, both for the training slopes in the Tyrol and in Switzerland, and it took the tactful persuasions of her mother, her mother-in-law and perhaps Aunt Joyce sympathetically pointed out the risks of a slip or a fall in the fourth month of pregnancy. The Duchess was if anything too cheerful about her baby; there was never a less nervous mother-to-be. "I shan't ski," she protested. "I shall only drift about, just company for Eddie." But she changed her mind at the last moment, and Princess Alexandra bore her off for a few days with the Myddeltons at Chirk Castle instead. When in London, the Duchess stayed at Kensington Palace with Princess Marina, while the decorators completed the overhaul of the kitchen wing at Coppins. But she celebrated her twenty-ninth birthday at Hovingham, where her husband dashed up to join her for the weekend and they enjoyed watching the first point-to-point of the season.

"She is looking prettier than ever," wrote a friend, a certainty the public saw for themselves when the Duchess attended a charity performance of "H.M.S. Pinafore" with the Queen. The prospective parents were also at the Savoy Chapel wedding of one of their close Army friends, Major Ian Baillie. With these exceptions. the Kents lived quietly. After his army driver had crashed the white Austin, the Duke drove himself to the office, and is said to have never missed a lunch-hour telephone call to his wife. During their calm and uninterrupted evenings at home, the Duchess had begun teaching him to play chess and he proved an adept pupil. An official caller noted with amusement not only the chessboard but also the current reading matter on the table, including two government reports on Uganda, and the Duchess smilingly explained, "I am doing my homework". The reason became evident in May when it was announced that the Duke of Kent would represent the Queen

at the Uganda independence celebrations in October, and that the
Duchess would accompany her husband.

Meanwhile, a new family group seemed already to be growing
around Katharine. In the early summer, Princess Marina and Prince
Michael came for weekends. In his second year as a Sandhurst cadet,
grown into a tall and handsome young man, Michael was taking
flying lessons at White Waltham and liked to pretend that the baby
would arrive for his coming-of-age in July. Princess Alexandra characteristically brought baby gifts back from everywhere she visited that
year, from Munich and Paris, Stockholm and Athens, and on Monday,
June 25th she was spending the evening with a friend when a
telephone call came in the middle of dinner. It was Princess Marina, in
great excitement, calling from Coppins. "Come at once," she said.
"Kate is starting to have her baby. And she needs all her family with
her."

Princess Alexandra arrived at Coppins just as Sir John Peel, the
Queen's gynaecologist, was leaving, and he shook his head smiling at
her expression of concern. It was, in fact, somewhat of a false alarm.
Sir William and Lady Worsley, who were also staying there, went to
bed no doubt thinking of that other troubled night nearly thirty
years earlier when Katharine had been born. Alexandra telephoned
the next morning to be told, "Not yet!" and the Duke decided to
go to his desk at the War Office as usual. Dr Stafford Saint, friend
and physician of the Kent family for many years, was indeed taking
morning surgery when he again received an urgent message from the
midwife at the house. He "got into his car at a run", just as the young
husband did a few minutes later in Whitehall. Sir John Peel and Dr
Vernon Hall, the anaesthetist, also hurried down from London. But
it was not until three o'clock that afternoon that "Her Royal Highness
the Duchess of Kent was safely delivered of a son", as the bulletin
announced. The Duke was so pleased, so jubilant and excited, with so
many telephone calls to make, that it took more than an hour to
agree the phraseology, which also added, "Both the Duchess and
her child are well."

Although the six-pound four-ounce infant was born tenth in succession to the Throne, he established a minor precedent in being the first
child born in the direct male line of the Royal Family to have no

princely title or rank, and so was technically a commoner. In July, 1917, King George V had decreed that his house and family should henceforth be styled and known as the House of Windsor, and in December, he further decreed by letters patent that the titular dignity of Prince or Princess and the style of Royal Highness should henceforth cease with the children of the sovereign and the children of the sons of any Sovereign. The stream of royal dignity thus ended with George V's sons and grandsons. The new infant was a great-grandson, endowed with his father's subsidiary title of the Earl of St. Andrews but otherwise, as the editor of Debrett pointed out, technically a "Windsor, Esquire". Coincidence trembled in the wings, for it was only by a narrow margin of choice that the child did not honour the Worsleys by being born a York. When King George V was choosing a family name, the title "York" had been considered and discarded. However, another link with the past was happily realized. When the Duchess of Kent was born, the local folk had sent flowers and plants from their gardens to the young mother. And now, in June, 1962, the members of the Iver Mothers Union picked roses from their gardens for the Duchess, knowing nothing of the coincidence, but thinking it a pleasant gesture on the birth of her son.

The fair-haired blue-eyed baby was baptised by the Archbishop of Canterbury in the music room of Buckingham Palace on September 14th and given the names of George Philip Nicholas. Technically royal or otherwise, he wore the christening robe of Honiton lace used by all royal babies and the ornate silver-gilt traditional royal christening font was brought up from Windsor. The godparents were the Duke of Edinburgh, Princess Alexandra, Lady Lily Serena Lumley and Oliver Worsley and, as at the Duke of Kent's own christening, the guests included the Queen, Princess Margaret, the Queen Mother, the Princess Royal—and the Coppins staff.

IV

Until their son's safe arrival, the Duke of Kent had kept from his wife his secret wish to learn flying. Such was his fond impression, although the Duchess drew her own conclusions from his eager interest in

Michael's experiences at White Waltham. Before he could take the course, however, it was found necessary for him to undergo a slight sinus operation. His wife visited him during his forty-eight hours in hospital, ragged him as a completely healthy fraud and gave the patient a favourable report on her own first addition to the new staff, the nanny, Mary McPherson, a girl from Aberdeen, formerly a nursemaid to the children of one of the Balmoral factors. Capable, resourceful, cheerful, Mary was to become a fixture of the Kent household . . . and the Duchess found her a dependable rock in the jittery moments whenever the Duke was taking a flying lesson and the telephone rang.

Everything went well, of course. The Duke counted himself fortunate in having his younger brother's instructor, Flight-Lieut. Derek Homer. Prince Michael had flown solo after only ten flying hours, but the Duke's instruction was more compressed in time so that he achieved his solo after only ten flying hours within twelve days. This occurred entirely within the rush of preparation for the visit to Uganda, which was to see Katharine also metaphorically gaining her wings, the first journey she was to undertake as a royal Duchess, playing her share of the dual role in representing the Crown. For the first time, she had the responsibility of choosing an expense-account wardrobe suitable for ceremonial drives and a State opening of Parliament, a garden party—indeed, a series of parties—a State ball, hospital visits, a "semi-safari and a demi-durbar". As is well known, the Duke and Duchess of Kent may submit expenses to the respective government ministry when undertaking a tour of duty on behalf of the Crown.* Princess Marina's secretary, Sir Philip Hay, steered the Duke through the financial preliminaries, while the Duchess sought the advice of the Queen—and her dresser, Miss Margaret MacDonald—in her choice of clothes. "It will be warm!" she was cautioned.

The Duchess elected to go to her wedding couturiers, John Cavanagh, and Belinda Belville, who had dressed her bridesmaids and pages. Miss Belville was nearly the same age as the Duchess, a factor in sympathy. Graduating through the worlds of dress manufacture and fashion editing, with little formal design training, it was only seven

* This was written before the 1971 review of the Civil List.

years since she had staged her first London dress show, borrowing her grandmother's West End flat for the occasion. Supplementing these couturiers with the millinery of youthful Paris-trained and English-married Jenny Fischer, whom she had patronised for some years, the Duchess was also effectively steered by Princess Alexandra to the wholesale showrooms of Susan Small.

John Cavanagh finds in his client an unusual quickness in explaining the basic things she likes and needs. Maureen Baker, her mentor at Susan Small, recognizes the Duchess's appreciation of line and simplicity and her skill in ringing the changes of an off-the-peg collection for the purpose in mind. For Uganda the Duchess sought deep and unusual colours, the probable preference of most of the people who would be meeting or seeing her. Her husband, too, was consulted on designs and fabrics, expressing an opinion with more wisdom and insight than the average male. The press meanwhile sought details of the Duchess of Kent's choice with eager interest and gave her appreciative coverage, finding no fault in her "uncomplicated elegance and youthful awareness". One paper irritably wished to know the number of pieces of luggage necessary for two weeks in Uganda but the Duke of Kent was practised in down-playing such details.

Royal visits have become a cliché to those who record the events of the monarchy, but there is always a first time, and the Uganda journey was to fill Katharine's mind with a wealth of close-packed impressions. She had been received aboard a plane of the Queen's Flight at a Yorkshire airfield on her honeymoon but had never before been the centre of a formal departure from London airport, amid salutes and presentations, boarding a royally refitted Britannia airliner. They winged away from the deep October clouds into evening sunlight and at 15,000 feet made a happy dinner party: the Duke and Duchess; Sir Philip Hay, veteran of many such journeys with Princess Marina; Lieut. Commander Richard Buckley, a young naval officer and distant kinsman who was soon to become private secretary; Lady Moyra Hamilton as lady in waiting and Group Captain Wallace.

In the morning, in the fierce sunlight of Entebbe, those who greeted the plane saw the Duchess "peering from the window like an excited schoolgirl. But the excitement, a high-pitched chirruping of pleasure, rose from the terraced rows of African women at sight of the Duchess "in a delectably crazy feathered hat and a bell-skirted silk dress in roaring sea green". The young Kabaka of Buganda, the Premier Mr Milton Obote, and the retiring governor, Sir Walter Coutts, and Lady Coutts formed the nucleus of the welcoming committee. And in the equatorial heat, driving to Government House past the colourful, chanting and—curiously—jumping crowds she forgot the sense of acting in an unreal pageant . . . and was delighted at recognizing that the thousands of decorative fronds along the route were banana shoots.

Their suite at Government House looked down the garden slopes to Lake Victoria. That evening they attended evensong at the Anglican church. Entebbe is the administrative capital and, next day, the Duke and Duchess drove by the perfect highway, never far from the lake-shore, to Kampala, the commercial centre, where they lunched with the Kabaka, made an intensive tour of the colleges and missions, schools and hospitals on the seven hills of the city and enjoyed the fantastic spectacle of a tattoo. The following day saw the Independence Day ceremonies, a reception by the Prime Minister at Parliament House and the State ball in the evening, when the Duchess looked truly regal in cream and gold embroidered organza. The Duchess danced with her Uganda partners, blonde-gold against brown and, while sitting out, tried to reply sincerely when guests asked what she thought of Africa. Yet how could one tell one's truthful impressions of that equatorial warmth, or equate the continuous welcome of drum-beats with the colour of streets and gardens in a land where birds are said to be bright as butterflies and butterflies big as birds?

If the Duchess surprised herself, it was in being taken unaware by the emotion that always underlies pageantry. When her husband, as the Queen's representative, opened the first Parliament of independent Uganda, and in his deep voice read the speech from the Throne, those close to her could see how deeply she was moved.

With the vast throngs at a garden party, all four thousand guests eager to see the blonde Duchess, this concluded the formal aspect of the visit, and the young couple's cameras were very much in evidence when they drove through the luxuriant eastern forests to see the massive wonder of the Owen Falls Dam, at the head waters of the White Nile, which the Queen had opened seven years previously. The barrage is a blinding white arc of concrete and foaming water half a mile wide, trembling and thunderous, so that it was almost a relief to escape to the different roar of the turbine room in the great power house. Then they flew north to Gulu to be deafened, thrilled—and incidentally half covered in ochre dust—at a display of tribal dancing. For the weekend they visited the Queen Elizabeth National Park where the Royal Safari Lodge had been made ready for their arrival. Major Kinloch, the game warden, had promised elephant and they awoke in the morning to find five browsing outside their bedroom window. On a land-rover expedition they photographed rhino, zebra, hartbeest and gazelle, a satisfying camera bag. For the Duchess, too, a satisfying conquest was in fact her first solo official engagement, on October 16th, when she opened the new Mulago Hospital in Kampala. Two days later, with her husband, she flew to Nairobi to open the new television centre and attend a cocktail party, and next morning they shivered in the late October chills of London.

V

The Uganda scene had been envisaged beforehand with fair accuracy but the future is seldom to be foreseen with such clarity. In all her anticipations of life with Eddie, Katharine had never imagined that she would celebrate her thirtieth birthday in a cramped upstairs army flat in Hong Kong, the fresh paint scarcely dry over the cracked plaster, and hardly room to dry the baby's washing on the little service balcony. Nor had she thought that in an attempt to join her husband she would find herself lost on a foggy November night in Essex, unable to find the airfield, with her plane due to take off within minutes, like an episode in a nightmare.

For the Duke Hong Kong was a fresh phase in his profession of soldiering. He had been posted to take up his duties as second-in-command of C Squadron of the Royal Scots Greys at the Sek Kong base in mid-November, and there were plans for the Duchess and their five-months-old son to fly out to join him at the end of the month. For Katharine it was another sequel in wifehood and of being in love. She knew that she would be travelling out with other wives and children in a normal trooping charter plane: with touchdowns nearly a two-day trip. Until the newspapers checked the passenger lists, she did not realize that the precise complement would be four babies, thirty children, thirty-six service wives and some forty other service passengers. "The baby will certainly sleep as far as Istanbul," she said with confidence.

Coppins was to be closed for eighteen months and, in the event, she left the house in mid-afternoon, and the fog instantly descended, so dense, so dark that it took four and a half hours to reach Kensington Palace on roads where they knew every yard of the way. When they again set out for Stansted airport, the baby, Georgie, the little Earl of St. Andrews, went to sleep in his cot on the car floor but, somewhere in Essex, the chauffeur had to admit that he had lost the way, and even the nanny, Mary McPherson, became flustered out of her usual calm.

They telephoned the airport to be told not to worry. The passenger coaches from London had not turned up, and the plane would be delayed. A resourceful officer booked the last two hotel rooms in Bishops Stortford for the Duchess, just in case. In fact, the journey was a disaster. Farther into Essex, on telephoning again, they learned that the plane had been cancelled and, turning back, they did not reach Kensington Palace until nearly midnight. Next morning, five mothers and children dropped out of the flight until the weather improved. But the take-off was planned, the Duchess set out, and this time the plane took off in early evening, "the sunset beautiful above dense white cloud", as one passenger wrote home.

Decidedly a royal duchess one day and an army officer's wife the next, Katharine thoroughly enjoyed the vivid contrasts. She had travelled to Uganda with Edward in the Queen's royally fitted Britannia, and now she travelled in the forward section of a Britannia under troop charter. Mary took little George back to the "baby's room" to prepare him for the night, but later, when walking along the aisle, the Duchess was torn between helping one young mother with a troublesome child or deferring to the stewardess who clearly wished to cope. As the papers said, she was certainly the first member of the Royal Family to travel on a women-and-children flight. But "K always has to beware of treading on toes", one relative wrote to a friend. The airliner touched down at Istanbul and Bombay, and

George gave little trouble. And then the plane tilted into the vistas of mountain slopes and wisp clouds and blue sea that spell Hong Kong. Every mother aboard was feeling a little deafened by the noise of children, and as the packed aircraft swooped onto the runway, Katharine saw Edward waving wildly from beside his Ford to gain her attention.

The adventure in the fog seemed already like a bad dream, but no doubt he teased her with not being able to manage without him. Castle Peak is a pleasant residential community on the Kowloon mainland, twenty miles or so east of the city, along a road spectacular with views of sea and hills and islands. Barbecue Gardens is an estate of white two-storey concrete army houses and, as they came into sight, the Duke pointed out a block with rounded concrete balconies—and this was home. Three days earlier, Katharine had been lodged in Kensington Palace. Now they climbed a concrete stairway to a small front door. The living-room had two wide windows opening on to verandahs, with wonderful views of ocean, islands and back-gardens. There were three small bedrooms, the largest not four paces by five across. But husband and wife were together with their baby—and a due share of the zest and beauty of Hong Kong.

The mess gave a party for the Duchess on the day after her birthday. The day itself fell on a Friday and was thus convenient for a private gathering at the flat, going out to dinner afterwards. With no children, their downstairs neighbour, Captain and Mrs Simon Cox, had more available space than the Kents and lent their spare room to Mary McPherson when the Kents needed to put up a guest. It was surprising how many friends from home visited Hong Kong in the course of a year, proving it indeed a main junction of shipping and air routes. Lady Anne Black, the Governor's wife, who gave a dinner for the Kents soon after their arrival, said with one of her droll smiles that she found it best to keep a running buffet at Government House. With many friends now among the R.S.G. wives, Katharine slipped into her own calm routine, wheeling George into a local park in the afternoons in his white pram, an unrecognized young mother in slip-slop sandals. She shopped with other wives at the military store, had tea with friends and joined in the birthday parties of other officer's families. Just as the Queen and Prince Philip look back on naval life in

Malta as an idyllic time in their early marriage, so the Duchess of Kent will always have a special affection for "the Colony". She and Edward went out only once or twice a week, and the Duchess and her nanny kept one another company in the empty interludes when the Duke was away on manoeuvres around Sheung Shui.

Once a week there were shopping expeditions into Kowloon or across to Victoria. On Sundays Edward "mucked in", as he said, at the Services polo matches and they pretended not to notice the social scalp hunting of such occasions. When Princess Alexandra's engagement to Angus Ogilvy was made public, the film renters offered the Kents a private showing of the engagement film but they preferred to slip into a regular evening show independently. The Duke of Kent was, of course, to give the bride away, and he overzealously allowed his days of leave to accumulate, rather than seek special privilege—in April, 1963—when they flew home to London for the wedding festivities.

The Princess met them at the airport, brighter and more irrepressible than they had ever seen her, her ebullient personality flowing over with abounding happiness. To Katharine it made a wonderful contrast to be in London again, the change of scene so swift and effective. One day she was shopping in Hong Kong and then, with no more than a weekend in the timelessness of flight, she found herself in Kensington Palace, in the familiar little flat, noisy with the chirping of London sparrows.

The two sisters-in-law went together to a fitting of the wedding-gown at John Cavanagh's salon in Curzon Street. Mr Cavanagh had specially commissioned a fabric from France for Princess Alexandra as he had for Katharine's bridal gown, but the material for the Princess was of the same mellow tone and traditional detail as a cherished family piece of Valenciennes lace which had been worn by her grandmother at her wedding. Katharine was utterly charmed, Alexandra had been longing to know her opinion, and the session ended with the Duchess taking away a generous clipping of the wedding fabric in her handbag.

Looking back, one sees in those years that the unusual sequence of royal marriages surrounded Katharine in a recurrent glitter of the happiest possible royal celebrations. We have watched Edward and his Katharine enjoying their own share in the dances and parties for Princess Margaret at Clarence House and Buckingham Palace. Now, for a third party scene, the Queen and Prince Philip gave a ball at

An Army wife arrived in Hong Kong. The Duke and
Duchess of Kent and baby son. (*Hong Kong Government*)

On duty—The Duchess meets provincial leaders
in Uganda, 1962. (*Keystone*)

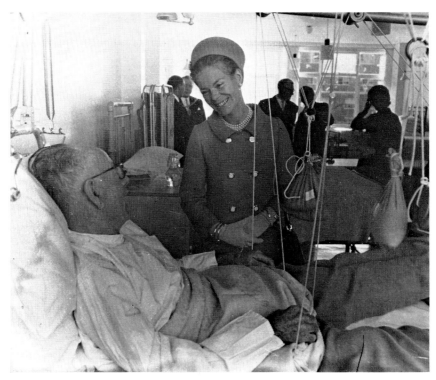

On duty—A smiling bedside manner when touring
a London hospital, 1969. (*Press Association*)

Controller Commandant of the Women's
yal Army Corps. (*Press Association*)

As Chancellor of Leeds University, the Duchess of Kent confers an
honorary degree upon her father. (*Press Association*)

th the children, 1966. The Duke and Duchess, Lady Helen Windsor
the Earl of St. Andrews. A study by Lord Lichfield. (*Camera Press*)

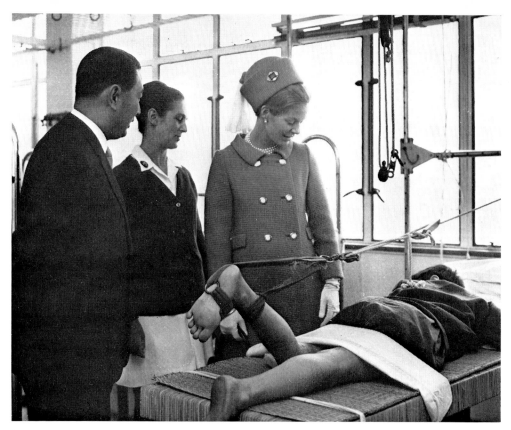

Morning in Hong Kong, at the Medical
Rehabilitation Centre. (*Hong Kong Government*)

Afternoon in Hong Kong, a housing visit on the
Wah Fu Estate. (*Hong Kong Government*)

e debut of Lord Nicholas Windsor. The Duchess
ves King's College Hospital with her second son,
y 31st, 1970. (*Press Association*)

The Kent family at Coppins. (*Camera Press*)

Windsor Castle, which was certainly the largest and most high-spirited party the old walls had seen for more than a century. The Life Guards' strings alternated with Joe Loss and with the pipers of the Royal Scots Guards for the Scottish dancing and, as I wrote later, those who saw it will never forget the sumptuous effect of the Waterloo Chamber, with its portraits bowered in flowers; and the brilliant and beautiful oval of guests around the gleaming floor resembled the splendid throng of an early Victorian ball in that very room, as depicted in a royal water-colour.

With the Royal Family and guests, more than seventy sat down to the private dinner beforehand, among them the King of Norway and his son, Prince Harald; Queen Frederika of the Hellenes with her son, daughter and future daughter-in-law; and the Queens of Denmark and Sweden, Queen Victoria Eugenie of Spain and Queen Helen of Rumania, surely an unequalled assembly in modern times. Afterwards, nearly a thousand couples came to the dance and, dancing together whenever they could, lost with one another in the crowd, it must have seemed to the Duke and Duchess like a renewal of their courtship: they were married, they had their little son—and here they were!

At Princess Alexandra's wedding, Katharine wore a coral coat and hat, the latter of distinctive Hong Kong inspiration, and watched with tenderness and amusement as her husband led the bride to the altar, a task he performed perfectly though with the utmost gravity. And if the Duchess looked pensive the moment the wedding was over, it was, I am told, because she suddenly began thinking of her ten-month-old George. It had been a difficult decision to leave him behind in Hong Kong, but babies do not take kindly to travel, and he was safe with his nanny, Mary, with the extra daily help of a Chinese amah. The only flaw of the wedding holiday had been Katharine's moments of taut anxiety at the thought of her baby half the world away. With the wedding over, she told a relative that she could hardly wait to get back to him—and it was wonderful indeed to find him chubby and so brown, moving around the room—the world's fastest crawler, as his papa said, a baby described aptly in the amah's own phrase, in Chinese dialect, "the little one with winged knees".

His first birthday, with one solemn candle, coincided with the fifth day of the fifth moon of the Chinese calendar and thus with the annual

6—TDOK

Taipo Dragon Boat festival. To help with the fun, his father volunteered for the twenty-six man crew of a British and Gurkha army entry. All went well, the paddles dipping to the beat of a drum, until the boat flooded and foundered with only the dragon's head and tail showing, and the crew swam alongside to complete the half-mile course by pushing the canoe ingloriously over the finishing line. The film of the ducking taken by the Duchess from an accompanying speedboat was to become what Prince Michael called a Coppins comedy classic.

The sequence had its counterpart in a movie taken by the Duke of his wife at a horse show. In the old days at York gymkhana she had gained local acclaim by jumping a small and fearless pony through a very large blazing hoop and the Duchess was sure that she could train an Army horse named Melody to undertake a similar jump in sensational style. Training Melody for the feat, and keeping up her riding, was a diversion with which she staved off the mood known to residents as Hong Kong boredom and the jump was performed perfectly on the day. For the Duke, there was also the Army rivalry of the go-kart races, of yachting with one of the 13-foot Enterprise craft of the army sailing club, and of water-skiing. There were occasional bouts of sight-seeing, notably a weekend spent with friends in Macao, and in October the Duchess wrote home delightedly to tell of the prospect of another baby.

10 The Royal Tasks

Close when I view thee Smiling,
Joys celestial round me move
Pleasing visions care beguiling
guard my State and crown my Love
To behold thee gaily shining
is a pleasure past defining . . .

Another song to Mr Handell's Minuet
(The January chimes)

I

The Duke and Duchess of Kent returned home to London early in December, 1963, home in time for Christmas as Katharine had hoped, and they paid a quiet family visit to Hovingham before going to Sandringham. The Queen's house-party at Sandringham House that year was one of the largest since the war and yet it was to be the last in the long unbroken chain of royal Christmas festivities in Norfolk, "Dickens in a Cartier setting", as it was once styled by the Duke of Windsor. The occasion was also notable for the presence of four expectant mothers—and indeed, five, when Lady Anne Nevill joined the house-party in the New Year. The four royal ladies—The Queen, Princess Margaret, Princess Alexandra and the Duchess of Kent—were resigned to laughing at mutual clumsiness and made a formidable group going out for walks together. The nursery group included young master George of Kent (the Earl of St. Andrews), Prince Andrew and Viscount Linley, all of whom joined the grown-ups for Christmas lunch. In the evening, glasses were gaily raised to the toast of "all the little strangers whom we know are present".

On the first big sporting day, the Queen and Princess Marina remained at Sandringham, but the Duchess went out with the other ladies who braved the chill and clammy fog to meet the men for lunch at the King's Head, that useful pub at Bircham. It was surprising how confident one could become between one baby and another, and Katharine did not believe in coddling herself for the newcomer. The only absentee of the Kent family at Sandringham was, in fact, Prince Michael, who was with his regimental ski team in Austria. His report on weather conditions was favourable and the Duke and Duchess joined him in St Moritz later in January for the British Army championships.

Regardless of the risk of slipping on some small patch of ice, the Duchess was confident that she could "sit about satisfactorily". Old snapshots and hotel flashlight photographs are all that remain of this holiday, as with so many others. Here is the Duke on skis starting off in the grand slalom; here a dinner-party with Stavros Niarchos; here Michael on the dance floor. Here is the Duke again . . . on crutches, his left foot swaddled in bandages, with Katharine offering a helpful arm. His ski-ing was perhaps rusty after Hong Kong. In a fall on the Corviglia slopes, he had sprained his ankle and tore two ligaments, and skied no more that season. "And to think you were worried about me!" said his wife, ruefully.

Claiming to be fit enough for desk work, the Duke joined his regiment in Germany when still walking with a stick. The Royal Scots Greys were now to serve a two-year stint with B.A.O.R., quartered on the little town of Fallingbostel, and Katharine flew out for her birthday weekend to help decide whether she should live at Coppins or in Fallingbostel after the new baby came. The hills still sparkled with snow, and indeed there was no question of not being with Edward, as Katharine told her family, if they were lucky enough to get married accommodation. It did not seem to occur to her that difficulties might melt away, and happily the outgoing tenants showed her around an Army house in Quebec Avenue which seemed to be ideal.

With this problem settled, she had no sooner returned to England than Princess Alexandra's baby son was born—arriving on Leap Year Day, February 29th—and Katharine joined Princess Marina in a visit to the handsome nine-pound six-ounce little boy, the first infant in the royal batch so fondly envisaged at Sandringham. The Queen's third son, Prince Edward, made his advent on March 10th and—

exceptionally—the Duchess of Kent was a godmother to both these royal babies of the year though present at neither christening. Hoping for a daughter, she anticipated that her own baby would be born in mid-May, but the Queen's gynaecologist, Sir John Peel, who attended the Duchess, hinted that the baby might be earlier, and so it proved.

Miss Howell, the midwife, moved into Coppins late in April and on Tuesday the 29th, the Duchess suddenly realised that her presence at Prince Edward's christening might be impractical. Her husband in Germany was alerted by telephone and gained leave to catch the first plane out . . . breathlessly entering the house, as one friend put it, only an hour or so ahead of the stork. As the bulletin said, "The Duchess of Kent was safely delivered of a daughter at 10.30 this evening. Both the Duchess and her child are well." The baby weighed seven pounds eight ounces, and Princess Marina expressed the contentment of both father and mother when she wrote to a friend, "We are delighted with my first grand-daughter, especially as Katharine longed for a girl."

Moreover, Marina could relate another wonderfully happy item of family news, for Princess Margaret's daughter, Sarah, was born that same week. The Princess had also planned to attend Prince Edward's christening with her husband but in the event Lord Snowdon was a alone, and Princess Marina deputized for the Duchess of Kent. Prince Edward, the Duke of Kent's namesake, was the first royal infant to be christened at Windsor Castle for many years and, at the font in the private chapel, the Dean of Windsor, then the Rev. Robin Woods, baptized the child as Edward Antony Richard Louis.

A chain of royal christenings now ensued. On May 11th, Princess Marina deputized once more for Katharine as sponsor to Princess Alexandra's son, James, in the private chapel of Buckingham Palace, the first baby boy to be baptized there since the war. Four weeks later, on June 6th, the Queen gave a very pleasant lunch party at Windsor for the Worsleys and other guests to precede the christening of Katharine's daughter, who was in turn the first girl baby to be christened in the private chapel of Windsor Castle in modern times. The sponsors were Princess Margaret, Mrs David Butter, Angus Ogilvy and Sir Philip Hay. Once again the Rev. Robin Woods officiated and the sweet and placid child received the names Helen Marina Lucy. To close the sequence, Princess Margaret's daughter was christened on July 13th, the venue this time being the private chapel of Buckingham Palace. As I have said elsewhere,* history may one day find romantic coincidence in these events.

II

After her daughter's christening, the Duchess of Kent remained in England only long enough to close up Coppins, and then slipped away with little George and the baby to join her husband in Germany without any fuss. The Coppins household played general post, for Russell, the steward, resigned to take up a catering career with a city staff canteen, while the Duke's then part-time secretary, Lieut-Commander Richard Buckley, moved into Mr Russell's cottage on the estate. The royal couple had to manage on the Duke's army pay and his investment income, not then implemented from the "supplementary provision" of the Civil List. Staff services had to be reduced or resumed as if at the touch of a switch, and Katharine's ability to look royal and yet "make do" was one of the factors that endeared her to the public. If it is true that part of the art of being royal is to maintain ordinary family life under extraordinary circumstances, the Duchess was beginning to feel an expert at it, and she comfortably set up house in Fallingbostel after making only a single journey to the shops.

As in Hong Kong, the Duke met his family at the airport—this time in his S-type Jag at Hanover—and they all piled into the car: Mary McPherson with the baby and two-year-old George at the back, and Katharine vivacious and excited as they set out on the autobahn. It is a paradox of events that the British Army of the Rhine is now centred 150 miles from the Rhine, in the vicinity of the Luneburg Heath, where peace was once signed and where the tanks now manoeuvre under N.A.T.O. obligations. By a fine irony, too, the British troops are stationed in that very region where the

* *The Married Life of the Queen* (1970).

British monarchy itself once changed direction, where the Electress Sophia walked in her garden knowing that her eldest son would soon ascend the English throne as King George I. But the Duke and Duchess of Kent, reunited again, were little concerned with such ancient things as they exchanged their news in the car. Susan, Aunt Joyce's eldest girl, was starting work in the stamp auction world and going on holiday to the Faroes; and now that her children were growing up or at school Aunt Joyce herself was taking up gliding at Sutton Bank.

The small town of Fallingbostel lies at the heart of the triangle of Bremen, Hanover and Hamburg, and is so full of British Army signboards that it half forgets to be German. Quebec Avenue is a tree-lined thoroughfare set with identical detached houses in German style which had been specially built for officers some ten years earlier. The Duchess had noted on her first visit that the entrance door was up four steps, which meant some difficulty with the pram; but the entrance was in fact at the side for added privacy, though the army families living nearby, those of majors and captains, the majority personal friends from both Hong Kong and Catterick, were incurious neighbours. The house had four bedrooms, with a garden large enough for a playpen and very little else. The furniture was standard issue, with extra chattels taken over as usual from the outgoing tenants. The Duchess changed curtains around, bought new lamps and cushions in a Celle department store—and within a week the house was "home".

The Duke was now regimental adjutant, and the spare bedroom ostensibly became a study, where he could work at his books in the evenings for his qualifying Staff College exam. Usually however, he preferred to work downstairs, where his wife often helped him by reading exam questions at random, a task she undertook with such mock sternness that the tutorial sessions ended invariably in laughter. The Duchess found herself becoming versed on military law, administration and morale, military history and tactical exercises; and two years later, when she became Controller Commandant of the Women's Royal Army Corps, she was by no means the green and inexpert honorary figure that the public imagined.

It was moreover one of the pleasures of the tight-knit regimental life of Fallingbostel that total strangers no longer pursued the Kents with invitations, camouflaged in good causes, as they had for a time in Hong Kong. The Royal Scots Greys was proud of being a regiment with a member of the Royal Family as a regular serving officer, on the job day by day, and the Duchess presented the sports day prizes, the gymkhana cups and the trophies of an inter-regimental flower show . . . it was all as pleasantly carefree as her Hovingham days. As at Hovingham, too, there were weekend invitations from friends and relatives who had been at their wedding: Edward's first cousin, the Graf Hans Veit of Toerring, for instance, and Prince Kraft of Hohenlohe, Prince Philip's nephew, who had only recently renovated a burned-out wing of his ancient castle and created one of the lushest modern homes in all Germany. As unusual royal visitors from England, the Duke and Duchess of Kent provided, in a sense, a dress rehearsal for the family visit of the Queen and the Duke of Edinburgh the following year, and it fell to the Duke of Kent, I believe, quietly and informally to clear up some of the local problems of protocol.

Often, too, there were weekends when they set off with a picnic basket like any other young couple to explore the countryside, the heather-clad heaths and wooded mountains of Lower Saxony, the valleys of the Weser and the west banks of the Elbe. The cities were less in their line, but the Duchess wrote of visits to Hamburg and Bremen, where she was unexpectedly charmed by old alleyways like the narrow streets of York.

She conscientiously began to learn a little German, useful on those purely maternal afternoons when she took young George to see the storks and parrots in the bird-park at Walsrode or indulged him with ice-cream in one of the pretty little tearooms in Soltau. Luneburg nearby is by no means an ugly army town but in fact a steep-gabled Hanseatic city with some pretensions to a spa. If, in the winter, the regimental life of Fallingbostel turned inward, Katharine was accustomed to the long Yorkshire winters, and the Kents counted themselves fortunate to have Christmas leave as well as a royal duty that took them briefly to warmer climes.

In a letter declining a royal patronage at about this time, the Duke explained that, while on military service, he could undertake public duties only as bidden by the Queen. The Christmas leave was lengthened by the Staff College examinations and then, on a dreary mid-February day in London, the Duke and Duchess flew to Bathurst to represent the Queen in the Gambia independence celebrations. The Duchess is said to have boarded the plane in a thick tweed suit and alighted in equatorial heat looking delectably cool in a summer coat and frock. The little Moslem enclave on the coast of West Africa—population 320,000—had not seen a royal visitor since Prince Philip called there on his 1957 world tour, and now the Duke and Duchess were received to the boom of saluting guns, to cheers from the crowds in the festooned streets and to garden parties black with smiling faces. Elaborate paper lantern parades were watched, schools visited, hospitals inspected, ceremonies performed, a seasonable change indeed from Fallingbostel.

III

The Duke of Kent served a total of two years in Germany, and was in married quarters with the Duchess for nearly eighteen months before they at last returned to Coppins in the early autumn of 1965. Their departure from Germany was marked by a champagne party in the mess for officers and wives, technically a delayed celebration of the 150th anniversary of Waterloo, as well as a homegoing send-off for the adjutant, and the Duke was able to celebrate his thirtieth birthday in his own familiar home. The recruitment of staff proved more difficult than expected, and for a time the Duchess ran the house single-handed, with only daily help from the village. This is an adjustment faced by every Army couple after a term overseas and, characteristically, the first indication that the Kents had really "settled in" was a nursery tea-party, with Prince Andrew, then nearly six, Prince Edward, their own two small fry and other children.

Undertaking a three-months military science course at Shrivenham, the Duke then lived in at the college and returned home only at weekends, itself a pattern of living familiar to army wives, while the Duchess picked up the urbane social threads of English life. Visits were exchanged, for instance, with Gerald and

7—[DOK • •

Angela Lascelles at Fort Belvedere, and with Alexandra and Angus at Thatched House Lodge. Lady Moyra Hamilton was another guest, and the Kents attended her wedding in Londonderry the following year. Katharine's father and mother also came to stay, exchanging Yorkshire mist for the wintry fog of the Thames Valley, and Sir William brought news of informal approaches that his daughter might care to become Chancellor of Leeds University. This was a signal honour, for the former Chancellor had been the late Princess Royal, and for a time this coloured the Duchess's thinking on the extent and regional interests of her probable public duties.

She was thus extremely diffident in accepting any office or patron-age that she considered might have been better offered to Princess Marina or Princess Alexandra, and anxious telephone calls between the Duchess and her sister-in-law on such points were not infrequent. She felt that she could fulfil some purely decorative functions such as attending the Rose Ball or the Royal Variety Performance with her husband, patronizing an official fashion show or opening a footwear exhibition, but when the Associated Fashion Designers of London asked permission to name her as one of the ten best-dressed women in Britain, a flurry of letters and phone calls was necessary before the Duchess agreed. There were fewer qualms in becoming patron of the Yorkshire County Cricket Club or of the "Not Forgotten" Association, with its charitable Service connotations, but one walked warily at times between the risk of seeming ungracious and the slightest hazard of family goodwill.

Happily, no considerations of this order marred Katharine's ap-pointment as Chancellor of Leeds University, the first such dignity conferred in her own right. Nothing spoiled the sparkle of the clear May day when she was to be installed, except the decision of some small part of the student body to demonstrate against the Vietnam war. Young men thus shouted and ran about the road outside Leeds Town Hall, placards and banners were waved and slogans chanted and drowned by counter-cheers. The Duchess took it all in good part, and the distant din during the ceremony of installation presently gave way to applause. Next day, all the newspapers carried a photo-graph of the new Chancellor, the youngest in the university's history, caught by the camera in one of her endearing comic quirks of expression as the tassel of her mortarboard cap drooped over one eye. The new Chancellor's first duty was to confer a number of honorary degrees and, the following year, far more by chance then design, it was her happy task as Chancellor to bestow an honorary doctorate of law upon her own father.

No doubt this shook the academic dovecotes, for such an event lacked precedent, except the similar occasion when the Queen Mother, as Chancellor of London University, conferred an honorary degree on Princess Margaret. "She has always bestowed love and affection upon me—why not a degree?" said Sir William in response to one questioner. In private, father and daughter were a little amused at the coming event, but on the day, during the ceremony, both were unexpectedly shaken by a tender emotion which neither quite succeeded in hiding, and it was only at the end that they broke into smiles. Again, in her role as Chancellor, it fell to the Duchess to confer an honorary degree of Doctor of Letters upon the King of Sweden. The ceremony took place in the Entrée Room in St James's Palace and in her robes in that ancient setting, with the portraits of great admirals to left and right, Katharine could sense what it might mean to be Head of State, involved constantly in such ritual in every imaginable form.

The realization of that ineffable task was to be brought still closer home on the eve of her birthday four months later. The Queen was due to undertake an Investiture of some of the 1967 New Year Honours, and at 10.30 a.m. the recipients were gathering in the Palace ballroom, nearly two hundred men and women with their close relatives, unaware that Her Majesty had been taken ill. In similar emergencies, Prince Philip has often taken over as deputy for the Queen but he was in the Middle East, the Queen Mother was convalescing from an operation, Princess Margaret was suffering from a chill and the Duke of Gloucester, though then in full health, was in Jamaica. The telephone suddenly rang at Coppins.

It was like any other domestic crisis. The Duchess telephoned her husband, now a temporary major, who was working in civilian clothes in an Army office in Hounslow. The Duke left at once for the Palace, normally a forty-five minute drive through crowded London. His wife meanwhile gave a final brush to his dress uniform an extra polish to buttons, an added sheen to his sword, and collected his medals. No Olympic baton was ever handed over faster than the Duke's uniform to an Army driver, and it safely reached the Palace only minutes after the Duke himself. The ceremony commenced— and the Duke, sword in hand, gravely invested the accolade of knighthood upon a lieutenant-general. Then, filing slowly forward, others came to kneel for the honour of knighthood or to receive orders and decorations. For more than three hours the ceremony went on, unhurried and personal for each individual, the Duke congratulating and shaking hands with each one after the bestowal, as the Queen would do. If it were possible, it increased his respect for his cousin, who faces the fatigue of such chores so cheerfully and so often. And the Queen had herself publicly indicated her regard for the Duke of Kent a few months earlier in his appointment as "personal aide-de-camp to Her Majesty", an honour he shares with Earl Mountbatten.

Safely recovered from what the doctors saw as an attack of mild food poisoning, the Queen telephoned birthday congratulations to the Duchess next day and added an honour that alone lay in her power to give, that of appointing her Controller Commandant of the Women's Royal Army Corps, with honorary rank as a major-general. The post had been formerly held by the Princess Royal, and at the birthday dance at Coppins that weekend the Duke joked that justice was done, for his wife now out-ranked him. Some people have been known to smile at photographs of the Duchess in uniform, and an honorary commission admittedly does not make a trained officer. But we have noted that, as an officer's wife, and the Duke's occasional exam coach, the Duchess's military knowledge and qualifications were in fact above average. At the commissioning ceremony at the Camberley W.R.A.C. College that summer, her salutes and her bearing were scrupulously correct and only her skirt length, a serviceable two inches above regulation, asserted a royal privilege to depart a little from strict Army standards.

The Duchess, in fact, consulted the Queen on the question of dress, clearly needing revision since the Princess Royal's time, and Norman Hartnell was entrusted with the new design of her bottle-green uniform. There were also tropical outfits, best seen in

February, 1970, when the Duchess undertook a solo tour of
W.R.A.C. and Army Catering Corps units in the Far East, a
journey remarkable for quite unexpected personal reasons, as we
shall see.

IV

Public and domestic events marched indeed in steady sequence as
the Duke and Duchess of Kent, in their early thirties, were increas-
ingly drawn into the magnetic persuasion, of royal duties. In May,
1966, for instance, the Duke represented the Queen at the independence of British Guiana—now Guyana—and the Duke and Duchess
left London airport with appropriate formality, attended by Lieut.-
Commander Richard Buckley, Group-Captain P. E. Vaughan-
Fowler, of the Queen's Flight, and with Caroline Douglas-Home,
daughter of the former Prime Minister, as lady in waiting. They flew
the Atlantic by BOAC Boeing, indulged in a free day on the
beaches of Barbados, then flew to British Guiana in an aircraft of
the Queen's Flight and spent a week in a wild mixture of calypso
and dignified ceremonial.

If the speeches were prolonged and sincere, the receptions humid,
the throb of the steel bands was irresistible and the dancing infectious. With her gift of looking cool and composed, the Duchess
watched with serenity as her husband read the Queen's message to
the Legislature; and the Guyanans were pleased that she admired
her husband "with much excitement" as he danced the famous
"jump up", leaping higher and higher at the State Ball. The royal
couple watched a water pageant on the Demerara river, made a
helicopter tour over the vast sugar estates of Berbice, attended huge
garden receptions, enjoyed the usual car cavalcades through avenues
of school-children, and indeed gave pleasure to the politicians of
both parties in what had been a troubled atmosphere. Then they
returned home in time for the York Festival, which Oliver Worsley
had long had a hand in organizing, and at Hovingham Hall Oliver
announced his engagement. He was in his fortieth year, and his
fiancée, Penelope Fuller, was only twenty-three. In many another

family, the age difference might have seemed to matter, but not among the Worsleys, with their happy example of Uncle Eddy and Aunt Joyce.

Next, in October, the Duke and Duchess flew to Lyons to inaugurate British Week. The royal sponsorship of these sales jamborees was then at its height; Princess Margaret and Lord Snowdon and Princess Alexandra had all been concerned in cities as various as Dusseldorf, Stockholm and Hong Kong and the invitation to the Kents arose naturally from the Duke's fluency in French and the involvement in the pageantry of the Royal Scots Greys. The Kents approached this task with such conscientiousness that they paid a private August visit to Paris beforehand to help brush up their French. The Duchess was determined to take Princess Marina's advice to "do everything thoroughly". The flocks of French journalists gained a news point when she went down on her knees to check the quality of a British wool carpet and, as for clothes among the fashion-conscious French, her first appearance in a coat of brightest yellow with a matching cloche hat helped establish, too, the resurgent prestige of *la couture Anglais*.

On their return, there was the pleasure of Oliver's wedding in Wiltshire, at which little George was a practised page, gaining compliments afterwards from the Archbishop of York, who had conducted the ceremony. The Earl of St. Andrews was indeed a sought-after page that year with his handsome looks, his fair curly hair, his deceptive angelic appearance. He had trotted sweetly behind Fiona Bowes-Lyon when she married Oliver's friend, "Joe" Goodhart, at Brompton Oratory and, if he broke into tears on that occasion, he was nevertheless on his best behaviour, a child from a Van Dyck painting, at Claire Pelly's marriage to Lord Herbert. If the Duchess of Kent looked fondly on her son on these occasions, she was fully justified. She had started him in music and movement classes in Iver village early in the year and had begun taking him to a nursery school nearby at Datchet that September, when he was already four. It illustrates the complex and affectionate family life of the Worsleys to mention that he attended school with a young cousin of the same age, Ralph Assheton, who was Marcus Worsley's nephew by marriage. Both small boys were pages to

Oliver's bride. And when the time came for the leave-taking, as bride and groom drove off from the lovely old Cotswold stone house, some wedding guests were puzzled at the Duchess's mischievous farewell cry to her brother, "We'll be seeing you!"

Yet the amusing coincidence of their birthdays seemed even now to work its magic again, for the newly-wed Worsleys honeymooned on Barbados and the Duke and Duchess flew there in November to represent the Queen in the independence celebrations. Duty and domestic events were thus linked once more, the processions and State receptions and speeches to Parliament threaded into the texture of lantern-lit private dinner parties, and Oliver's joking protests that he could not get away from his kid sister, even on honeymoon. Barbados is, of course, also the stronghold of the Lascelles sugar estates, and behind the outer formality of the constitutional changeover there was the warmth of many personal friends whom Katharine had long known. The table-talk was a soufflé of topics, of point-to-point and of George commencing riding lessons on a Shetland pony named Lucifer and unexpectedly producing juvenile abstract paintings at school. It could be said, too, that he was a great plane-spotter, devoted already to model aeroplanes. Among the jaunts of the year that cropped up in conversation, a two-week holiday on the isle of Elba appeared to equalize with the pleasure of taking George plane-watching one afternoon on the roof terrace of London airport.

Not many months later, a dance at Coppins for the Duchess's thirty-fourth birthday saw a procession of the more privileged guests who tiptoed into the nursery for the pleasure of peeping at the sleeping children, George and two-year-old Helen. This might have happened in any home, and yet we may contrast this domestic vignette in turn with the chief official role in which the Kents were concerned in 1967 when they represented the Queen at the coronation of King Tupou of Tonga. Many of us remember the laughing, uninhibited figure of the Queen of Tonga who so nearly stole the show during Queen Elizabeth's coronation procession drive in 1953. Now she had been succeeded by her equally tall and statuesque son; the coronation festivities were to last for a week with all the magnificent liberality of Tongan tradition, and the

Queen and the Duke of Edinburgh clearly felt that the Kents had earned this opportunity of experiencing South Seas fun.

The Duke and Duchess flew out to Fiji with Richard Buckley and Fiona Pilkington. The international date line turns Greenwich midnight into Pacific high noon, but they seemed "quite unfatigued", a Fiji official wrote at the time. "They spent part of their intended rest time snorkel diving." The visitors had seen the films taken by both the Queen and Prince Philip, but were unprepared for the astonishing sounds of Tonga, the haunting serenade of the nose flautists, the magnificent hymn-singing. They had received royal warning however of the pyramids of food that would confront them.

"You must eat up," the Queen had told Katharine. "They may be disappointed otherwise." The feasting was to last for a week, the daily banquet was estimated to run to one thousand pigs, one thousand heads of poultry, fish and fruit in untold abundance and the sacrificial splendour of dozens of turtles transformed into soup. The Duchess is at best a sparse eater and a film show shows her seated on the ground outside the royal pavilion, tucking with a will into lobster and yams, vast slices of melon, long slivers of pork, and chicken ripped Tonga style with her fingers. Probably only a coronation, Tonga fashion, could have equated with the enjoyment she knew she was missing of George at his first school sports day, and George sturdily playing the part of a gnome in the end-of-term play.

No one had studied the Duke and Duchess's Pacific itinerary more keenly than John Worsley in Toronto. If one family pleasure could not be pursued in those halcyon days, there was still another enjoyment that could be. By changing planes they could stop over in Toronto and see John's new apartment on Dale Avenue and, more important, his farm near Uxbridge some sixty miles from Toronto, the estate he had named Stockingtop, after the peak of Hovingham High Wood. But best of all Katharine could catch up with the children: Willa, now twelve, Harry aged nine, and the two youngest, Jonathan and Dicken, whom she had never seen.

John as usual managed everything magnificently, whisking his visitors through Toronto airport so adroitly that few realized royalty had arrived. Brother and sister were amused that the one now lived just north of Uxbridge, Ontario, while the other at Coppins was just south of Uxbridge in England. And Stockingtop was truly a discovery, a two-storey log-cabin of the old colonial days surrounded by apparently limitless acres. To the original log and shingle farmhouse, John and Carolyn had added two brick-built wings: a large bay-windowed living-room with a familiar water-colour of Hovingham Hall to lend a theme to the pale green walls and, on the other side, a combined kitchen and family room, with a hanging rope-ladder and swing for the children reminiscent of the gym at Castle Howard. The improvements still in hand progressed a stage farther with Eddie helping John to build a wharf to the excavated pond that formed a swimming-pool, while the children took their aunt on a review of the rabbits, pet pigeons, chickens, guinea-fowl, horses, steers, lambs and other agricultural populace.

Talking, sun-bathing, swimming, savouring the tangy contrasts of South Pacific and rural Canada, the private days passed delectably, and it mattered little when the local girl reporter tracked them down. They went on to friends in Muskoka, the William Balfours, who had a cottage on Lake Joseph, with the added diversions of sailing and water-skiing. Though Muskoka has no mountains to set off its lakes and rock and pine, the northern atmosphere vividly reminded Katharine of her stay at Banff and Lake Louise—was it really eight years ago?—and her longing to share it all with Eddie. If she confessed as much to John, he seemed to pay very little attention. The presence of the Kents in Canada was now widely known and, concluding with a visit to the Hardinges in Montreal, they added their names to the roster of royalty who had toured the world fair wonders of Expo. But John gave one of his most quizzical smiles in saying goodbye—and certainly it was no coincidence, before that sparkling summer ended, that the Duke and Duchess of Kent received an invitation to open the Calgary Stampede in the following year.

V

Looking forward to rewarding work and play alike, the Kents thus ushered in the New Year of 1968 in the usual way at Coppins with no presentiment of the changes hanging over them. John's Christmas card, with a drawing of Stockingtop, stood on the mantelshelf bright with promise. Princess Marina and Prince Michael were due to leave on a three-week safari visit to Kenya and Uganda in February, looking with heightened interest through the photographs that the Duke had taken in Uganda five years earlier. The year was foreseen as one of customary regimental routine for the Duke, and for the Duchess a not too onerous quota of royal duty. She was, in fact, increasing the broad spread of her interests at a measured tempo, in February assuming the commitments that would come of linking herself as a Life Member with the Women's Section of the British Legion, and in March consenting to become patron of the Nuffield Orthopaedic Centre. In May a brief round of official engagements was made to Northern Ireland. But in July the week's visit to Calgary was treated as a glorious lark, an overweek outing, a private fun visit concentrated into seven days leave.

Laughter began in their suite at the Pallister Hotel as soon as they saw the headline, "The Kents Hit Town". For the one rip-roaring week of the greatest outdoor show in the world, as Calgary boasts, the city trebles its population to a million, the streets packed with pseudo-cowboys, and the Duke and Duchess entered into the spirit of the thing. The Duke declared the Stampede open and, seated cross-legged upon a bear rug, he was initiated in an Indian ceremony as a honorary chief member of the Blackfoot tribe. If the Duke had reservations on being named Ah-tsee-ta-mukka, meaning Running Rabbit, it was gravely explained that the rabbit was the only animal the eagle cannot catch and, more suitably, the Duchess was named Ah-nah-dakee, meaning Pretty Woman, while the onlookers roared their approval. In all her dream pictures of Eddie of long ago, Katharine had not imagined him in Indian gear joining uninhibitedly if briefly in a war dance. Watching the junior steer wrestling and decorating, the chuck-wagon races and other events, she said "I can hardly talk with contentment".

Over the weekend, in the sharp air of the Rockies, showing her husband the peaks and precipices, the canyons and churning white torrents in the Banff and Jasper national parks, the dream now forged into reality must have seemed at the time a rounding-off, a completion, of all the chapter of years since that first separation from Eddie before they married. And then, back in town, as if in a jubilee, they rode western style in the Stampede parade, preceded by the big band of the Irish Guards and followed by a squad of Mounties. As Ian Brodie cabled home, "Running Rabbit and Pretty Woman rode into town in Stetsons and cowboy gear while 200,000 palefaces roared approval. Said Pretty Woman, 'I'm shaking with delight'." It was like riding in a circus parade in brilliant sunlight, their saddle-cloths proclaiming "H.R.H. The Duke of Kent" and "H.R.H. The Duchess of Kent" to ensure that no one missed recognition, through five miles of acclaiming cheers and the blare of bands. They waved arms and called responses to the crowds until throats ached. The Duchess had rarely felt so carefree in her life. Returning home, they were full of Stampede stories, matched by Princess Marina's animated account of the Wimbledon tennis championships at which she had presented the prizes.

Princess Marina's left leg was however paining her, causing a tendency to stumble. Making light of the trouble, she thought that she had rheumatism but was persuaded to enter hospital on July 16th for an examination. Six days later she returned home, having been advised to rest and take a course of electrical treatment. She was not told that she had an inoperable brain tumour; and it fell to the Duke of Kent to tell his brother, his sister and his wife of the doctors' terrible verdict that Princess Marina had at most only six months to live.

The physicians counselled her not to take her usual holiday in Italy with her sister, Princess Olga, and her children's first thought was to cancel their own holiday plans, only to realize that this might indicate to their mother the seriousness of her illness. Princess Alexandra and her husband had planned to spend two weeks in Sardinia. They thought it best to go but reduced their absence to a long weekend, pleading Angus's excessive pressure of business. The Duke and Duchess of Kent similarly stayed with Vincent Poklewski-Koziell in Sardinia, telephoning Princess Alexandra nightly to ensure that all was well. Their late summer schedule of engagements was drawn up in the usual way. But Princess Marina was to be spared a long illness. On August 24th, the twenty-sixth anniversary of her husband's death, she said prayers for him during a brief service and spent a tranquil and happy day at Kensington Palace. The next morning, she said "I feel tired. I think I will go to sleep," and from that sleep she never awakened. She died the following day.

Katharine was at once the strength of the family, the solace and resolution of her husband and Prince Michael and Princess Alexandra, who felt her mother's death so deeply, and of Princess Olga, last of three sisters who had played so happily at Tatoi so long ago. Giving one another mutual encouragement, the Duchess of Kent and Angus Ogilvy in turn were thankful that the autumn programme of engagements was a therapy to occupy them all. It was what Princess Marina would have wished.

11 Today's Duchess of Kent

How does my love pass the long day?
Does Mary not tend a few sheep?
Do they never carelessly stray . . . ?

The Tweed Song
(The August chimes)

I

Only three women, technically commoners, have successfully married into the British Royal Family in the past century.* The first was the daughter of the 14th Earl of Strathmore, the present Queen Mother, who married the then Duke of York, second son of King George V, in 1923. The second was the former Lady Alice Montagu-Douglas-Scott, daughter of the 7th Earl of Buccleuch, who became Duchess of Gloucester when she married George V's third son in 1935. The third exemplar, today's Duchess of Kent, is of course the only woman to have emerged to popular celebrity in this way since the second world war. And if Miss Katharine Worsley, on becoming a royal Duchess, could still have remained honoured but unsung, inconspicuous and unknown, she would have nevertheless merited public interest as the only unadorned "Miss" to assume the mantle of a princess by marriage since perhaps Tudor times.

Historians, taking their wider perspective, may one day regard the first seven years of the Duchess of Kent's married life as a chapter in itself, a prelude spent like the Queen Mother's first early royal years in the calm of married happiness and motherhood, with only gradual training in royal experience. The Duchess of Kent's first seven years were however strangely sealed by Princess Marina's death. A page had been turned, and the chapter was closed. As a young wife and a tyro royalty, Katharine had always lived, like a child in lamp-light, in the brilliance of Princess Marina's lustre. Then suddenly the radiance was

* We exempt marriages overseas.

gone, and in that dark instant Katharine was the *only* Duchess of Kent.

As recently as 1966, a national opinion survey statistically assessed Princess Marina as "a favourite royal person, charming and unaffected, regal and dignified, a help in modernising the monarchy and sharing the burdens". The Duke and Duchess of Kent, on the other hand, were found to have "apparently made little impact as yet . . . the couple are not very well known". In her own terrain of public responsibility, the young Duchess tended her own small candle, never wishing to dim, far less compete with, Princess Marina's effulgence. Inaugurating a Yorkshire television station, she shrugged off a bomb scare and said, "One gets used to these things!" but she confessed privately that she still felt "the merest beginner" in royal engagements.

She made presentations, visited hospitals and schools, opened homes for the blind, and presided over the Christmas parties of the Not Forgotten Association in the Riding School of Buckingham Palace, as if at Hovingham Hall. But the limitations and restraints that she imposed on herself as if in deference to Princess Marina were as real as if they had been written into her marriage contract. For her part, Princess Marina was always pleased at any complimentary reference to her daughter-in-law and would often draw admiring attention to some new Press photograph. Yet Katharine herself could never quite believe in the legend of her own popularity. The Duchess of Kent of whom she read in the newspapers had never quite lost the mantle of fable. The cameras were focused upon the idea of royalty rather than upon herself. At the theatre one night, watching an understudy who was suddenly called to stand-in for the star, she said, sympathetically, "I can understand how she feels".

Only two weeks after Princess Marina's passing from the scene, there occurred however the curious incident of a royal non-event that indicated the Duchess of Kent's willing and unreserved acceptance of all the demands and responsibilities of her royal vocation. The *Court Circular* of September 15th contained the announcement from Coppins, "The Duchess of Kent was present this evening at a Soirée held at Sutton Place, near Guildford, in aid of the Royal Academy of

Dancing. Miss Fiona Pilkington was in attendance." But the bulletin had been prepared and issued ahead of time and in reality the event never took place.

The evening saw the climax of days of heavy rain when floods inundated Surrey even to causing loss of life. Around Guildford many roads were impassable and some of the approaches to Sutton Place disappeared under three feet of water and mud. It was clear that many expected guests at the charity dinner would not be coming, but when Lady Bellinger, the organizer, telephoned Coppins she found that her principal guest was fully prepared to set out. "If you decide to carry on, I shall certainly come," the Duchess assured her. When everyone realized how widespread and serious the floods had become, the soirée was cancelled, quite literally a wash-out. But the Duchess had shown determination and readiness in face of the odds, as a citation might say, and of course when the function was eventually held, she turned up without the smallest hint of domestic difficulty in fitting in the extra engagement.

In February, 1969, the Duchess of Kent began to assume eight of the various patronages and other offices formerly held by Princess Marina, more than doubling the commitments she had at that time, and to these she added, also, some of the patronages of the ill and stricken Duke of Gloucester. If she had been diffident before, now she could not do enough. A royal patron has always been something more than a name heading the office notepaper, a gracious presence accepting bouquets at a charity dance or perhaps making an occasional inspection of head office or home. But the work that the Duchess of Kent puts in can be judged by a cross-sample of her activities for one society alone.

A ready illustration lies in the Spastics Society, which has established well over 100 schools, training centres, clinics, workshops and residential homes and hostels for spastics and finances medical research and training projects for the handicapped to the tune of about £2,000,000 a year. The Duchess of Kent agreed to become Patron in succession to Princess Marina in February. In May, she visited the London head office to meet the directors and staff and acquaint herself more thoroughly with the details and scope of organization and then went on to visit one of the central London employment and family service centres. In October, she flew to Colchester to open and tour a new spastics residential centre, to make a speech and unveil a commemorative plaque but, above all, to talk to the workers and residents, admiringly to watch how one woman, unable to use her arms, can type invoices with the aid of a plastic stick held in her teeth, how a handicapped girl can weave footstool seats with her feet, how others can operate a loom despite the handicap of twisted and distorted hands and arms, and so forth.

The Duchess compassionately saw courage in being, and kept it in being by herself becoming a subject of conversation for days. In November, 1970, she visited Chertsey to open and tour a new children's treatment unit, making a stimulating and encouraging speech which, as before, gained wide publicity for the cause. In December, she attended a carol concert at the Royal Festival Hall to benefit spastics, an occasion still more important because it was broadcast and helped to raise £3,000 towards funds. Such artists as Moira Anderson, Vera Lynn, Sir John Gielgud, David Kossoff and many others had given their services and it was the Duchess's smiling task to thank them and accord them approval and gratitude in turn and, again, the resulting publicity all helped to focus national attention upon spastic needs.

Two months later, in February, 1971, the Duchess visited the Society's paediatric research unit at Guy's Hospital, drawing public attention to the £2,000,000 research programme into the causes of cerebral palsy. The following month, in visiting the Ideal Home exhibition she made a special point of calling at the Spastics Society stand and in May, 1971, she opened a new purpose-built spastics school, therapy and occupational centre in Exeter. "It is challenging work which grips the imagination," she said. And the Exeter visit was similarly stretched to the full by including a visit to the local residential home of the Distressed Gentlefolk's Aid Association and a call at the Exmouth branch of the National Life-Boat Institution.

The Nuffield Orthopaedic Centre then engaged her attention and, having accepted the patronage, the Duchess of Kent presented the annual nursing prizes one year, opened new wards another year and in 1971 helped to observe the centenary of the Headington Centre by attending a commemorative church service and a garden-party. Add patronage to patronage, engagement following engagement, and one begins to discover the constant task work of preparation behind the scenes as well as the continuity of involvement. Becoming the patron of St George's Hospital, she created a field day for patients by touring the hospital only two weeks later.

It is instructive also to study the roster of what the Duchess deprecatingly calls one of her "rather busy spells", a typical three weeks in December, 1970.

Nov. 11: Travelling in an aircraft of the Queen's Flight to visit the Salisbury General Hospital and Salisbury Youth Activity centre.

Nov. 12: Attending a Director's conference of the Women's Royal Army Corps at Lansdowne House.

Nov. 13: Visiting a spastic treatment unit. (A typical moment: encouraging a handicapped ten-year-old in the swimming pool. "Can you swim? Show me what you can do?" Pause as the Duchess kneels beside the pool, regardless of splashes and puddles. "You did eight strokes, that's very good.")

Nov. 14 and 15: Weekend free.

Nov. 16: Attending the 140th anniversary dinner of the Royal Geographical Society, and presenting the Society's Gold Medal to moon-traveller Neil Armstrong.

Nov. 19: Opening a new Radiography centre at the Royal South Hampshire Hospital, a visit to Brookside Training Industries at Southampton and attending an evening diplomatic reception at Buckingham Palace.

Nov. 23: Admission to the freedom of the City of London and luncheon with the Clothworkers' Company and Dyers' Company at Clothworkers' Hall.

Nov. 24: Opening antiques fair for the Arthritis and Rheumatism Council. (Incidental detail: kneeling down to receive a bouquet from a child who had newly learned to walk.)

Nov. 25: Presenting long-service badges to district nurses at a ceremony at the Drapers' Hall.

Nov. 26: Visiting the University of Leeds as Chancellor.

Dec. 1: Opening the new Science Block and Library at the Royal Masonic School for Girls, Rickmansworth.

Dec. 3: Opening a new Dental Hospital and School in Glasgow and visiting a Scottish newspaper office.

Not arduous but continuous. Thanksgiving services in St. Paul's Cathedral, launching ships on Teeside, attending Red Cross centenary parades, presenting medals for lifeboat heroism, inaugurating old people's homes, viewing fashion shows and art exhibitions held in aid of charity. Some occasions of comparative boredom (although the Duchess never shows it) such as opening an international trade congress, some evenings of pure pleasure such as a charity gala performance at Covent Garden. And through it all a striking ever-changing variety of dress ensembles that attract instant press attention and implicit publicity for the good cause she is serving. Through each successive programme all her smiles, vivacity, eagerness, interest and helpfulness, a star pupil indeed for her early mentors, Princess Marina and the Queen Mother. A complete and successful royal graduate.

II

Across the level plains of day-to-day engagements, the occasional journeys overseas rise—even for the most travelled royalty—as enjoyable peaks of fresh incidents and impressions. In 1969, the Duke and Duchess of Kent were appointed to visit Australia, New Guinea—where the Duke was to open the South Pacific Games at Port Moresby—the British Solomons and the New Hebrides, an opportunity they welcomed with verve and pleasure. A little more than a year since their visit to Fiji and Tonga, the tour was a token of that earlier success but, for the Duke, it was also a journey threaded with sentiment and signposted for them both with future prospects. It was just five years since Princess Marina had visited Australia, returning full of eagerness that they, too, should have the experience "like being in quite another world". It was thirty years, also, since the Duke's father had been preparing for a term as Governor-General, that never-fulfilled mission, and now, at Government House, Canberra, the Duke and Duchess could still feel his "Coppins influence", expressed in the blue satin-clad sofas, English curtains and panelled or painted off-white walls that he had chosen.

Princess Alexandra, ten years earlier, had delighted in the pastoral views, still not greatly overbuilt. But travelling royals these days tend to be like flying businessmen on ever-tighter schedules. The Kents had only a weekend sightseeing in Canberra, mingled with church-going and official duties such as wreath-laying at the War Memorial and visiting the city-planning centre, before they flew to Port Moresby. And here the Duchess found her husband steeped in nostalgia once again, the scenery and atmosphere so strongly remindful of his first royal tour with his mother, to Malaya and Borneo, when he was still only sixteen. The atmosphere was indeed very different. They found Port Moresby crowded with young athletes from every corner of the Pacific. But when they flew overland to the more tribal atmosphere of Vunakanau, past and future seemed almost to merge in the vortex of time.

Yet, again, things were different. The Duke was to have thanked the tribesmen for their welcome, but in protest against some political issue, the chieftains did not appear, and his wife's eyes twinkled as she listened to his hurriedly reworded speech. Royals nowadays take the rough with the smooth. On flying to Darwin two days later to commence a tour of the Northern Territory of Australia, they were greeted at the R.A.A.F. base with a twenty-one gun salute and the immense hospitality of the families of the Air Force personnel. For the Duchess, it proved a time for remembering the children, the berry-brown youngsters whom she met first in their homes and then at school, the skilful self-assured happy family group at the cattle station at Brunette Downs where they spent a weekend—and where the fair English Duchess startled the youngsters not a little by showing that she, too, could rope a steer.

Then there were the aboriginal children at the mission on Bathurst Island. Tom Wilkinson, of the Darwin radio, inveigled the Duke into a studio interview in which he said that frankly he would like his son to come to Australia, either during schooling or later. The Duchess sat by and watched, but went on the air herself the next day at Alice Springs to talk to the outback children over the School of the Air network. "My own son and daughter at home know about your schooling," she told her audience. "They think it a wonderful idea. I think they imagine that you just sit back in armchairs and allow the teachers to do the work. But it isn't like that, is it?"

The Australians had discovered by now that "two unusual royals" had arrived, and a wider welcome next awaited the Kents in Adelaide. The Duchess as always responded with enthusiasm and tried to do too much in the humid heat. On arrival in Perth, she had to see a doctor who diagnosed exhaustion and prescribed rest. Striving not to miss anyone, she had talked to too many people, stood too long at the civic receptions and too willingly prolonged the programmes of touring hospitals and schools. But if she was temporarily barred from receptions and church services and saw little of Perth, she visited Geraldton on time the following day, visited the prosperous fruit belt of the Chapman Valley and spent the Saturday morning on programme, trudging around the iron-ore mine at Mount Newman.

There's no duty more demanding and exigent than royal duty. "Of course, it's nice to carry on," she said. "I feel quite better." Yet the problem was to arise again more sharply six months later. If wishing can make it so, she had wished to share something of her husband's knowledge of Singapore, and February, 1970, saw her scheduled to undertake her own first solo tour overseas. Visiting an Army Catering Corps training centre at Aldershot as Commander-in-Chief, she had put on a comical look on seeing a well-laden display buffet and joked, "I should do this more often". And when a proposal arose, the comment grew into a tour of W.R.A.C. and Army Catering Corps units in Singapore and Hong Kong.

She was due to fly out on February 9th. Shortly after Christmas, however, she made an unexpected discovery which Dr Saint at Iver duly confirmed. A baby was on the way, perhaps in July. The idea of a pregnant Colonel-in-Chief may have appealed to her sense of humour but she refused any hint the tour might be postponed. The visit, she protested, could not be strenuous, she would be at home with the Army and in good hands: there would be no harm to the baby in walking around Victoria Barracks.

The evening after leaving London, indeed, the Duchess was enjoying a sightseeing drive around Singapore in highest spirits, as if oblivious of the sudden transfer to equatorial heat. She arrived in tropical white service dress, was greeted by the Commander-in-Chief, Middle East

Forces, and eagerly began her programme the next morning. Sheaves of Army photo contact prints, as well as signals home vividly recapture her impressions: the military car cavalcades, the arrivals, the presentations, the salutes, handshakes, conversations, barrack inspections, the canteen and kitchen scrutiny, the visits to office switchboards and courier services, the Duchess constantly smiling, questioning, setting others at ease, and passing on to other inspections, conversations and pleasantries, in that atmosphere, unavoidable, of spit and polish. After four days, the royal party flew on to Hong Kong in an R.A.F. VC 10 to the same duties and atmosphere renewed, a free day spent with Sir David and Lady Trench at Government House, a day with the Army, and a day of civilian duties. The official army signals merely listed four engagements, but in reality the doctors of the medical rehabilitation centre in Kwun Tong welcomed her to the wards at ten a.m. The centre is concerned with the rehabilitation of the handicapped and the Duchess toured the physiotherapy rooms, the occupation therapy departments, the X-ray rooms, even the surgical appliance workshops for artificial limbs. In the wards she went from bedside to bedside "with a smile and a word of cheer to all". Then in the morning sunlight she walked to the Princess Alexandra School for Crippled Children, touring classrooms, handicraft studios and the staff living quarters, missing nothing.

Back to Government House for lunch and then a tour of the Wah Fu housing estate in Aberdeen, where the accompanying reporters delighted in her visit to the tenants in an eighth-floor flat. The Duchess then toured the play area of the estate, the market, the boys and girls clubs and a kindergarten, thus engaging public attention for the need of such amenities elsewhere. Then followed a drive to Sandy Bay to visit the children's orthopaedic hospital and, again the leisurely, watchful progress through every department, the staff not a little astonished at her practical knowledge.

This is royalty in action, in effectual public service regardless of self. The Duchess of Kent flew home in time for her thirty-seventh birthday and was still working through her schedule of engagements the following month when her expectation of a third child was announced.

III

"Kate needs all her family with her," Princess Marina had said, in summoning Princess Alexandra when the first baby was born. In 1970 the Duke of Kent had just begun a six-month tour of duty with the Royal Scots Greys as a unit of the United Nations peace-keeping force in Cyprus and the arrival of the third child was quite without fuss. Sir John Peel, the gynaecologist, arranged for the accouchement at the King's College Hospital in South London; the Duchess entered hospital on the Friday evening and gave birth to a six pound four ounce boy on the Saturday night of July 25th.

There was nothing unusual except the Duchess's determination to tell her husband the news herself. She was indeed so concerned about it that a telephone call was promptly put through to Zyyi camp near Limasol and "happy and not too tired" she spoke to him that same night.

The infant was the first male of the royal House of Windsor to be known as Lord Windsor, and one doubts whether any child, born thirteenth in succession to the Throne, ever made an advent with less nonsense or formality. Nanny McPherson brought eight-year-old George and six-year-old Helen to see their new brother at the ordinary visiting hours the next day and, on leaving hospital five days later, cradling her baby in her arms, the Duchess seemed surprised at the waiting posse of photographers. The chosen names, Nicholas Charles Edward Jonathan, were made known with little delay and the infant was baptized in the Private Chapel of Windsor Castle on September 11th, with the Vicar of Iver assisting the Dean of Windsor.

An amusing circumstance was that the baby seemed to coo with alert pleasure at the singing of the choristers of St George's Chapel, and an unusual—perhaps unique—feature was that the father stood proxy for the Archbishop of York as sponsor. Prince Michael also stood proxy for the Duke's great Goodwood friend, Lord Nicholas Gordon-Lennox. The Royal Family were then in Scotland but Prince Charles flew down from Balmoral to act as chief godparent. "You sponsored me—I'll sponsor him," he said, as a sequel to the ceremony earlier that year when the Duke of Kent, with the Duke of Beaufort, had introduced the Prince of Wales to the House of Lords. And then there were the three smiling godmothers, Lady Susan Hussey, Lady Cecil Kerr and Mrs Alan Henderson, not only close personal friends, but also all three steeped auspiciously in ideals of royal service.

Lady Susan Hussey, daughter of Earl Waldegrave, is for instance a lady in waiting to the Queen, particularly on call for informal youthful occasions such as centenary visits to schools or children's hospitals. She was formerly an aide to Princess Anne and from time to time deals with the Queen's correspondence from children. Lady Cecil Kerr, a daughter of Lord Lothian, has a lively optimism, public zeal and widely informed Parliamentary knowledge that at times must remind the Duchess of her more youthful self. Fiona Henderson has often "attended the Duchess", as they say, and was lady in waiting on the Kents' 1969 visit to Australia and on the Duchess of Kent's Army visit to Singapore and Hong Kong. Uncomplicated, good-natured, idealistic, unselfish, tactful, discreet, versed in the needs of the Court, the present-day personality of the Duchess of Kent may be divined in this coterie of close friends. And to these one may add Miss Jane Pugh, (daughter of Lady Musker and step-daughter of Sir John Musker, the banker) who was appointed lady in waiting in July, 1970.

Three days after the christening of baby Nicholas, the Duchess launched afresh into her public engagements by opening a fashion show at Dunkeld to raise funds for cancer relief and research. Two weeks more and she flew to Toronto, with Jane in attendance, to inaugurate a United Appeal for seventy-five participating charities. John Worsley had once unerringly attracted Katharine by promising to show her his children. Now she had a family of her own, and, as organising chairman of the United Appeal, he lured his sister just as decisively by the good she could do for charity. She found it "a fun visit" in the sheer enjoyment of again seeing John and Carolyn and their children from Willa, now fifteen, to her two-year-old namesake, Katie. But the fun visit included the necessity of being briefed at the Appeal offices, of lighting a torch at the appeal opening ceremony, of being the centre figure of a civic reception, a luncheon, a tea-party of community leaders and a public dinner. The following day saw visits to a day nursery, a Jewish home for the aged, an institute for the blind and a boys club, where the Duchess was inveigled into showing her worth at table tennis.

In a smaller, more limited way Toronto saw all the hustle and activity of a royal tour, all the handshakes, the constant smiles, the conversations with hundreds of people. For John and Katharine, as two people, brother and sister, it was fun and fatigue and purposeful fulfilment. John made 160 speeches in the course of the campaign, and told friends afterwards he felt totally whacked. But only the day after returning from Toronto, his sister officially visited the Yehudin Menuhin School in Surrey and so began a freshly energetic programme for October that included opening a new county hall in Bedford, opening a new school in Bournemouth, inspecting a civic development scheme in High Wycombe, a ship-launching in Middlesbrough and a commemoration service at the Royal Hospital, Chelsea. Between her October and November activities, the Duchess sandwiched a flying visit to her husband in Cyprus. A well-earned few days, one may think.

Yet this is the delegated work of monarchy focused in effective action. The Queen cannot do everything. She cannot begin to recognize every industry, show support for every good work or even visit every foremost hospital more than once or twice in a lifetime. The Queen Mother cannot step into every breach in the great meshwork of social enterprise. Among the women of the Royal Family, Princess Anne, Princess Margaret, the Duchess of Gloucester and Princess Alexandra strive in turn to spread the embroidery of patronage and interest. In terms of rank, today's Duchess of Kent is the seventh lady of the land. In present-day terms of royal duty, though still so modest and unassuming, she is fourth from the Throne itself.

The Kents also illustrate the routine task-work of monarchy at its least extravagant, most simplified and, cost-wise, probably most effective. As the reader may know, the Duke and Duchess received no fixed annual provision in the Civil List, and they were not included in the message to Parliament in which the Queen sought reconsideration of royal finances. It may appear a strange omission in view of the duty done. The Select Committee of 1952 stopped short down the scale of the foreseeable succession after lavishly recommending £35,000 a year for the Duke of Gloucester. There remained only a Supplementary

Provision of up to £25,000 a year to pay the expenses of persons, not otherwise provided for by Parliament, to perform royal duties on the Queen's behalf. And to this was added an illiberal clause that any balance left in one year should be retained and accumulated. There should in fact be no productivity bonus, no rewarding largesse. It was rather as if a car manufacturer were attempting to run the production line without paying the workers.

The Duke and Duchess of Kent are reimbursed for the salary of their private secretary, Commander Buckley, and his invaluable office assistant, Miss R. A. Oliver. They can recoup a stipend for Sir Philip Hay, in his role as treasurer of official duty expenditure. Cash is refunded against certified accounts of such expenses as postage and stationery and occasional car hire, as well as a small percentage for hospitality incurred on the Queen's behalf. Yet the Kents tend to underplay rather than indulge their expenses. The Duke of Kent does not charge the cost of his evening limousine as Grand Master of the Freemasons, an office he agreed to hold partly because his father had been Grand Master before him. The Duchess did not charge any costs for the United Appeal in Toronto. She can regain a minor proportion of Jones', her chauffeur's, salary but, scrupulously, not the proportion presumably utilized when Jones takes her daughter by car to day school at Datchet.

The Earl of St. Andrews now goes to Heatherdown, the Berkshire prep school selected by the Queen and Prince Philip for Prince Andrew and perhaps in due turn for Prince Edward. This has the advantage of sharing in Prince Andrew's police security, but the school fees of £200 per term must involve the Duke of Kent in stern financial reality. From his basic army pay (of about £3,000 a year before tax) he meets the basic domestic and living expenses of Coppins. Houses and cottages on the estate, formerly used for his mother's staff or for family friends, are leased off, one to a Harley Street surgeon, another to a well-known actor, to help meet expenses. And accounts would clearly run into the red but for the Duke's private income of about £4,000 a year, derived originally from the funds bequeathed in trust by his father.

Enigmatic factors similarly intrude in the Duchess's own account books. Her constant charming changes of wardrobe, immaculate to the smallest button, suggest heavy dress bills as well as an impeccable fashion sense. To eyes appraising accessories, millinery and shoes, there is the hint of a private income, perhaps deriving originally from Brunner funds. The expenses of a wardrobe created especially for a royal tour seem properly within Supplementary Provisions. There are ball gowns of striking colour and exotic appeal, serving their purpose at independence ceremonies and functions, and never seen again in softer climes. Yet for the majority of her engagements, the Duchess's dress expense remains her own affair, within her own income, freely spent though it is upon the royal cause.

As the Court Circular announcements so often say, "The Duchess of Kent today visited . . . Her Royal Highness, who travelled in an aircraft of the Queen's Flight, was attended by Miss Jane Pugh and Lt Cdr Richard Buckley, R.N." She travelled effortlessly indeed in a helicopter, taking off from the Coppins paddock. She was met on landing by the Lord Lieutenant of the county and the Chief Constable, with their cars lending the impress of a royal cavalcade. Whether for hospital or welfare organization, she would no doubt later meet the High Sheriff, a mayor, a chairman, a director, a warden or matron or two. And the smooth running of the day's programme had involved Commander Buckley in paying a prior visit to help plan organize and advise, with not infrequently a rehearsal visit by the lady in waiting. She in turn is on a provisional salary, entitled to travelling expenses but seeking them rather too seldom. She is the quietly dressed girl in the background, the Commander's right-hand in stage-managing the day, and she too is usually someone of private means who would blush to be awarded a dress allowance and is there, like the Duchess, for the sheer virtue, pleasure and exhilaration of the job.

IV

Like the longcase clock on the staircase at Hovingham Hall, Time itself rings the hours, the days, the decades, with pleasant ever-changing variations. Nearly forty years ago, when little Katharine Worsley took her first tender steps on the cricket lawn with her brothers, the former Duke of Kent, her husband's father, was living at

York House, St James's, with his eldest brother, the Prince of Wales. It was from here indeed that he left for his wedding to Princess Marina and had to dodge back on discovering that he had no money in his wallet. York House is a part of St James's Palace and stands in Ambassadors Court, in the cloistered heart of the Palace buildings, as if at the nucleus of royalty.

Queen Mary's grandmother, the first Duchess of Cambridge, had once lived there, presiding like a deity over all her descendants. Queen Mary herself made her first London home there as a bride. "Very pretty, such fine lofty rooms!" one of her relatives exclaimed, on first seeing this "gorgeous new abode". Yet when the then Prince of Wales—later Edward VIII, the present Duke of Windsor—decided to rehabilitate it as his London home, he found it, as he says, "a rambling antiquated structure, a veritable rabbit warren, with passages inter-rupted by unexpected flights of steps leading to unsymmetrical rooms full of ugly furniture." This was exactly fifty years ago and all the intense public loyalty and affection around the Throne was concen-trated upon York House as its more cumbersome wings were divided off into offices, and its amenities heightened to improved standards of modern comfort.

In the knowledge and good taste of renewal, the late Duke of Kent became his brother's chief adviser and he was given a bachelor foothold there in a two-room suite of his own. With the Abdication, the Duke and Duchess of Gloucester were granted the occupancy of York House as their London home and, in the melée of redecoration, a map studded with the red-topped pins of royal engagements long hung there as a symbol, one of the last relics of the old regime to be taken down. To this day, the old-fashioned London lamps above the portico of York House are topped with golden crowns and a guards-man of the Household Brigade stands sentinel at the door. "It is like an assortment of college buildings clustered round a group of small courtyards," a former occupant once wrote of St James's Palace. "Although so near to Piccadilly a special sort of quiet hangs over it." It is a peace so strangely deep at times that when the Duchess of Gloucester recently moved to Kensington Palace she found herself disturbed by the chirp of sparrows.

The Queen knew that York House had become too large for the

needs of her aunt and in 1969 she offered Princess Marina's old home at the corner of Kensington Palace to the Gloucesters, while the Duke and Duchess of Kent were offered the grace-and-favour lease of a reconstituted suite in York House itself. The Duke of Kent naturally felt the atmosphere of Kensington to be tinged with family sadness, however pleasant the change of identity when the Duchess of Gloucester moved in her things. He retained no more than an office suite, with the familiar old 937 phone numbers. But 1971 found his wife full of new plans and ideas for their *pied à terre* in York House, her spare hours in London often preoccupied with the Ministry men, involved in a series of decisions on how the residence might be cut down in size. There would be space for a number of various departments of the Lord Chamberlain's Office to be effectively rehoused. The Central Chancery of the Order of Knighthood could be brought under the one roof instead of occupying rented accommodation in Buckingham Gate. By 1973 the scheme will provide much-needed extra space for the Garden Party Office, the Surveyors of Pictures and Works of Art and the Marshal of the Diplomatic Corps, busy royal departments whose ramifications remain all too little known to the public.

The Duchess of Kent's friend, Dr Ramsey, once said in similar context that at Lambeth Palace he lived in four rooms. "The rest of the place was what? Secretaries' offices, reception-rooms . . ." At York House the Duke and Duchess of Kent will occupy a seven-room suite, consisting of a sitting-room, a small dining-room, a study, and four bedrooms—with space that serves to embellish the national status they have gained by merit.* The natural light wood walls of the entrance-hall seem to echo the Dukes of Kent, father and son. A formal ground-floor room has been reviewed in its utility for entertaining Commonwealth guests from Marlborough House, which stands, so to speak, next door but one. The four bedrooms foreshadow space also for Princess Alexandra's needs when wishing to stay in town with her husband, and town space, too, for Prince Michael, whatever his future felicity. When the work began—in March, 1971—friends who went shopping with the Duchess found her glowing with the needs of others, as her dream plans near completion.

* Yet the Kent apartment costs only £11,000 of the total £147,000 estimates.

As I write these concluding lines of our interim biography, Annigoni is commencing the preliminary studies for his portrait of the Duchess of Kent, amid the domestic seclusion and tranquillity of Coppins. This, too, is her life, with her love of husband and children balancing the need of incessant activity perhaps inherited from her mother, her vivacious personality difficult for a master to define in formal portraiture.

In seeking to depict the personality of his sitter, seen with an artist's intuitive vision, Annigoni always recognizes the intangible moment when a third person interposes in a portrait, "a third person", as he says, "with the most secret countenance of the model". In his pursuit of the inward Duchess of Kent, he will surely find the child who ran her errands about a Yorkshire village, the schoolgirl who rode theatrically red-cloaked to Castle Howard, the determined fledgling of Oxford and London, the daughter of wealth who worked in an orphanage, the girl of simple heart who gave her love to a prince . . . and perhaps most of all the descendant of the Worsleys of all the centuries who found scope freshly to interpret in royal ideals the profound promise of the Worsley family motto, *Quam Plurismis Prodesse*, the greatest good to the greatest number.

The Patronages and Official Connections
of H.R.H. the Duchess of Kent

Arthritis and Rheumatism Council
British Epilepsy Association
British Legion Women's Section (life member)
Buckinghamshire Association of Youth Clubs
Buckinghamshire Branch of the British Red Cross Society
Derwen Training College for the Disabled, Oswestry
Distressed Gentlefolk's Aid Association (President)
International Social Service of Great Britain
Iver Fair (joint patronage with the Duke)
Kent County Playing Fields Association
National Old People's Welfare Council
National Society for Cancer Relief
National Women's Auxiliary of the Y.M.C.A. (President)
"Not-Forgotten" Association
Nuffield Orthopaedic Centre, Headington, Oxford
Professional Nurses and Midwives Conference
Robert Jones & Agnes Hunt Orthopaedic Hospital,
    Oswestry, Shropshire
Spastics Society
St George's Hospital, S.W.1.
York Civic Trust
Yorkshire County Cricket Club

Women's Royal Army Corps—Controller-Commandant
A.T.S. and W.R.A.C. Benevolent Funds (President)
Women's Royal Army Corps Association (President)
Army Catering Corps—Colonel-in-Chief
Yorkshire Volunteers—Honorary Colonel
The Royal Australian Air Force Nursing Service—
    Air Chief Commandant

Leeds University—Chancellor

City Livery Companies

Clothworkers Company
Dyers Company
Company of Glaziers and Painters of Glass